C
HARMONY

ANARCHIC HARMONY

THE SPIRITUALITY OF SOCIAL DISOBEDIENCE

WILLIAM J MURRAY

LOOMPANICS UNLIMITED
Port Townsend, Washington

This book is sold for information purposes only. Neither the author nor the publisher will be held accountable for the use or misuse of the information contained in this book.

Published by:

Loompanics Unlimited
P.O. Box 1197
Port Townsend, WA 98368
Loompanics Unlimited is a division of Loompanics Enterprises, Inc.

Cover by Stephen Barnwell

ISBN 1-55950-082-4
Library of Congress Catalog Card Number 91-078422

CONTENTS

When nature's way was lost, honesty was invented.
When honesty was lost, laws were invented.
   — **Lao-Tse, *Tao Te Ching***

You can't have everything. Where would you keep it?
   — **Adam Weishaupt, *Konigen, Kirchen und Dummheit***

INTRODUCTION
by Robert Anton Wilson

This wonderful little book by William Murray offers a brilliantly vitriolic analysis of the confusions, superstitions and anxieties that make us all slaves *part* of the time and make most of us slaves *all* of the time.

If you stop and think about it, our slavery is the strangest, weirdest, most mysterious thing about us. After all, we are alive 200 years after the Declaration of Independence and over 100 years after the Emancipation Proclamation. Yet if you get ordinary people drunk or stoned, and encourage them to express their inner emotions, most of them will immediately admit they hate their lives because they spend almost all their time doing things they loathe.

How could this happen? How could we fight for liberty in one revolution and insurrection after another, from the Dark Ages to now, and then forget what liberty means? By raising this question, Murray confronts the most serious problem on this planet — the problem that most psychologists, sociologists, and other behavioral scientists prefer not to look at.

Consider the "ethical" teachings of our alleged sages and gurus.

F or the last 4000 years — at least! — these "prophets" have arisen periodically to teach, in essence, "Do what *I* will shall be the whole of the law." (Obey me. Don't think.) All of these Law-givers quickly acquired huge followings of disciples and launched movements that swept across the world murdering everybody who didn't believe in their dogmas. Only after millenniums have rational critics dared to ask why the hell we should all do what these "prophets" tell us to do; and such rational criticism remains a dangerous profession even today (as witness the death sentence against Salman Rushdie).

Early in this century, another "prophet" (or anti-prophet) arose who taught, in opposition to all tradition, "Do what thou wilt shall be the whole of the law." (Don't believe me. Think for yourself.) He was immediately denounced as a villain and a monster — "the most evil man in the world," one tabloid said — and still remains the single most controversial figure in the history of religion.

Comparing the careers of those who taught "Do what I will" as against the one heretic who taught "Do what thou wilt," it seems evident that humans possess a strong desire to be told what to do (and what to think) and an equally strong fear of anybody who tells them to decide for themselves.

If Hilter was a politician of genius, as many historians claim, what does that tell us about politics and about political society? His whole career was based on the theory that "the masses are female" and want to be dominated by the kind of "alpha male" who rules a baboon pack. If Adolph's analysis was not largely true, how did he, starting out as a nobody with no capital, manage to become total dictator of a nation the size of Germany? Did you ever try to become a dictator of even a single city block? It isn't easy — unless you do understand mass psychology.

After decades of mulling this mystery — why people are so terrified of freedom and so eager to have somebody else tell them what to think and what to do — I sometimes think I finally found the answer in the 18th Century Neapolitan sociologist Giambatista Vico, best known today as the inventor of what we call transpersonal linguistics. Vico had lots of other ideas, however, but wrote them in rather opaque language — in Naples, at that time, the Holy Inquisition still occasionally toasted people who had original notions.

Vico seems to imply, in his indirect Neapolitan way, that the earliest divinity was the thunder, and morality derives from traumatic experiences with thunder (i.e., "negative imprints"). Vico was the first to study the cave peoples (and also proposed that "Bigfoot" was a survivor of that age, a theory still popular in some circles). From cave art he deduced that anything that happened just before thunder was construed by our hominid ancestors as arousing the anger of the thunder-god.

Thus, imagine some cave man about to clunk his brother on the head with an ax — something most children still try once or twice, with the deadliest implement they can find, before their parents "cure" them of such tendencies. Vico's hypothetical Dawn Man was about the bop his bro (cf. Cain and Able) when the thunder suddenly crashed. For the next 30,000 years we have kept the taboo, "Never kill members of your own tribe."

War goes on, I guess, because in those early days the thunder never struck when somebody was getting ready to hit a "damned foreigner" (non-tribe-member) with an ax. Ergo, people still don't feel much dread or guilt at the thought of killing people from outside their tribe. (In fact, they usually celebrate it with parades and marches and songs, etc., like a malign fiesta.)

Similarly, some delightful sexual dalliances got put under Big Taboo, because just as somebody was trying them, the sky roared again. It must have been frustrating in the extreme: "Oh hell, we can't do it that way after all." Another taboo lasted 30,000 years or longer...

n some cases, nobody could figure out what had provoked the anger of the sky-god — why the thunder roared at a certain moment. The early shamans must have given this a lot of thought. They finally decided that since nothing had happened, the god must have gotten royally pissed off at something somebody *said.* And so, bit by bit, or byte by byte, more and more ideas and images were denied verbal expression, because the thunder-god might get into a frightful snit if he *heard* them being uttered.

Thus, we still have long lists of unspeakable words and unpublishable ideas, because the old brain, where primitive imprints are stored, still fears that primordial thunder-god (*who appears, incidentally, on the sound track of almost every horror movie*, when the director wants to activate our deepest collective anxieties).

Even people who think they have outgrown the thunder-god and the taboos of the Old Stone Age will find certain atavistic fears creeping up on them, in some modern works of art which deliberately violate taboos and conventional ways of thinking. Sen. Jesse Helms — who is financed by people who make a living literally poisoning us with the killer drug, nicotine — can always grab the headlines by finding a new work of art which might activate the wrath of the Jewish Thunder God, Yahweh.

We live in a world in which most people decide most questions on the basis of such brilliant propositions as "It must be true because the Vatican says so," "It must be true because the Central Committee of the Party says so," "It must be true because the Committee for Scientific Investigation of Claims of the Paranormal says so," *etc., etc., ad. naus.*

If you fear Blasphemy and Heresy — if you think certain ideas and images can be dangerous to us, that they can literally bring down "curses from heaven" (the roars of the Giant Thing in the Sky) — this book can be extremely hazardous to your health. If you are in the censorship business, perhaps the safest course is not to read the book at all, and just issue a general condemnation of it based on your ideas about what might be found in here if you dared to read more than 5 or 10 of the eldritch and unhallowed pages that follow.

(Incidentally, there is a clergyman at large in this great nation who claims that Mister Ed, the talking horse on the TV comedy, is the Great Beast foretold in the last book of the Bible. Is this rev. gentleman joking? Are you quite sure about that?)

Of course, at times I suspect that Vico's thunder-god, like the Marxist surplus labor, Freud's primal patricide, Velikovsky's great comet, etc., is just another iconographic myth — a structural analysis or model of our human predicament, rather than a literal explanation of its historic origin. It doesn't matter. Each such myth sheds a different and interesting light on the primordial riddle of "this sickness called humanity" (Nietzsche): why are we, unlike any other animal, alienated from our own instincts?

Mr. Murray illuminates how this system of alienation is passed on from one generation to the next, and he eloquently depicts how it cripples all of us. To borrow a metaphor from one of my own books, we are giants forced to live in houses built for dwarfs, and we have all developed a psychological crouch as a result. The irony and pathos of our situation lies in the fact that, mostly, those who crippled us did it because they loved us. You can't think about this deeply without wanting to laugh or cry — or do both.

One of Murray's stories reminds me of my own life: my mother told me that I didn't have to work on the docks like my father, but could get an education and work in an office. I told her I wanted to aim higher than being a drone in an office; I wanted to become a writer — which means being self-employed. She said that was very dangerous, because most writers starve to death.

I was too young and ignorant to reply that everything worth doing is very dangerous and can result in starving to death and in worse — in every other punishment society inflicts on the nonconformists.

Well, I spent 20 years working in offices. Twice I thought I had enough in savings to risk taking 6 months off and writing full-time. The earnings were so meager each time that I rushed back to the first job I could find after the 6 months of "dangerous freedom" ended. At 40, I could stand it no more. I quit another job and kept on writing full time, even though I did use up my savings and went broke in less than two years. I had to go on Welfare for over a year, then — an Infernal abyss of grinding poverty and anxiety — until my writing did begin to support me and my family.

(I love to tell this story, because it acts as an Ass-hole Detector. Those alleged libertarians who use this experience of Welfare to attack me as "immoral" I classify as Terminal Ass-holes and not worth debating with. It saves me a lot of time and energy.)

Fear and mental laziness, we have long known, are the major causes of conformity and slavery. Less recognized and even more pernicious, however, are the conditioned *guilt* and *shame* that keep us locked up in the same "mind forg'd manacles" as all the other workers, drones and soldiers in our human ant-hill. Virtually no libertarians dare to challenge the basis of this guilt-and-shame complex, because that involves challenging our deepest anxieties and taboos... (think again of the thunder-god on the movie sound track...). Max Stirner, Friederich Nietzsche and Aleister Crowley (the "Do What Thou Wilt" chap) were among the very few who did fight this issue openly and boldly, without euphemisms or evasions. William Murray with this book joins that very small, elite group of true Revolutionaries.

*There lives more faith in honest doubt, Believe me,
than in half the creeds.*

— Tennyson, 1809-1892

*Ask, and it shall be given you; seek, and ye shall find;
knock, and it shall be opened unto you.*

— Matthew, 7:7

Liberty consists in doing what one desires.

— John Stuart Mill, 1806-1873

"WHO THE HELL DO YOU THINK YOU ARE, ANYWAY?"

What credentials must one have to understand the principles that form and drive creation? How many Ph.D.s are necessary, how many years of counseling and therapy to unlock the secret of our own identities and our purpose in the universe? Can modern man claim a greater perception of reality or better qualifications for understanding our existence than primitive or savage man?

What qualifies a person like me to write about such concepts? All I claim is to have been born with an innate sense of *doubt* and *curiosity*. Growing up, I couldn't understand *why people did and believed what they did.* I marveled at the wide variety of belief systems in effect on our planet, and the irrational way in which people clung to those beliefs, as if they were deathly afraid of being without them.

I didn't understand why money was so important, why individuals I came in contact with would suffer any abuse or physical malfunction to keep their job, advance their career, and become a "success," miserable or not. We all grew up trained to be searching for "true love," to get married, have a family, and pursue the "American Dream." Everyone was willing to make themselves *miserable* in this insane search for *happiness*, as defined by our socially perpetuated "truths."

Yet those that attained various levels of this program of success and family weren't any happier than anyone else — as a general rule — regardless of their position on the economic and emotional ladder. I wondered, if certain "things" are supposed to make you fulfilled and happy, why didn't it happen with greater frequency when those "things" were attained?

It also seemed to me that mankind was the most destructive, useless, and ineffective species on the planet, and I wondered if perhaps the two were somehow related; could man's inability to accept and understand the nature of the world around him be at the root of his personal and environmental dilemma? Was this pursuit of the American Dream somehow putting him at odds with the forces of nature, causing his physical and psychological disharmony?

Looking around, we seem to be the only creatures, the only *entities*, no matter how complex or simple, that cannot, by and large, live in harmony with the rest of the planet. *Everything else*, whether it be "alive" or "inert," fulfills a purpose and is a harmonious part of the whole.

What's our problem?

We're constructed pretty much like other animals that inhabit this world, consume and excrete similar products. We're made of the same materials and are born and die similarly to other creatures. The only difference one can find is that we *consciously and subconsciously evaluate, modify, and restrict our interaction with the world*. Apes, which are creatures almost identical to us in every physical way, have no problem interacting harmoniously with the natural world, never giving a thought as to the ramifications or subjective value of their actions — and you don't see them extinguishing other forms of life, destroying their environment, or going crazy because of psychological difficulties. If every other form of life and "inanimate" object is capable of harmony *naturally*, then surely we, with our great intelligence, can sort it out.

Or can we? Isn't it that *intelligence* that requires us to evaluate our desires according to a societal set of "rules" before we take action in the world? Isn't it that *intelligence* that runs us through the endless corridors of justification and guilt after we take any action, causing us further modifications in our behavioral patterns?

The world and universe around us is constructed to be completely *user-friendly* — operable through instinctual and built-in guidelines. The dumbest animals have no trouble whatsoever in fulfilling their various purposes in the scheme and chain of life. It is like a well-designed radio; the on/off switch is clearly marked, the tuner dial is conspicuous, the volume control obvious. Even if you don't know the language, a few seconds is all that is required to understand the function of the equipment — unless you stubbornly *believe* the controls to be a certain, set, *other way*. Then trying to get the radio to work is just an exercise in fruitless exasperation, ultimately destructive to both the radio and the user.

Mankind refuses to perceive the true nature of the radio, demanding that it work according to the societal rules he has been programmed with. We, being part of the universal "radio," are like transistors that refuse to believe they are transistors, and behave according to a made-up, arbitrary set of rules that prevent us from fulfilling our purpose in the radio. The radio isn't working properly, and we are unfulfilled and frustrated.

This is where all other life-forms on this planet are one-up on us; they accept life and reality *the way it is*, without question or misinterpretation. And so they can live in harmony, reacting instinctually to events as they occur, according to the true nature of the situation. Since mankind is so inefficient and destructive, it must be because he *believes himself and creation to be something other than what is truly the case.*

It doesn't take being a quantum physicist to understand reality, it just takes a little objective observation. It sounds almost silly, but *the design of reality and our purpose in it* is inherently simple and straightforward and is completely apparent to anyone capable of a little honest self-examination.

What prevents us from honestly observing creation are our own self-imposed limitations and the "knowledge" that society has programmed each of us with so completely, indoctrinating us into its inefficient, destructive mythology. We feel we don't have the ability, in a world of experts and specialists, to figure life out for ourselves. Our own ability to understand the nature of our existence appears trivial in the modern world of Hubble Telescopes, electron microscopes, particle accelerators, and gene-splicing. Who are we to question the structure of so wise and advanced a society?

What I found by turning my back on our society-generated mythology was so profound that I had to share it — presumptuous or not — because it *indicts the social structures of mankind* and *demands social disobedience*, or living according to our inner, *heroic* nature and *not* according to the intimidation and demands of society's ineffective ideology.

But when you think about what people are actually undergoing in our civilization, you realize it's a very grim thing to be a modern human being. The drudgery of the lives of most of the people who have to support families — well, it's a life-extinguishing affair.

— **Joseph Campbell, *The Power of Myth***

Man was born free, and everywhere he is in chains.

— **Jean Jacques Rousseau, 1712-1778**

SOCIETY AND REALITY

In the counter-culture revolution of the '60s, there was a lot of talk about the "system," the "establishment," or, more intimately, the "man." Exactly defining what these labels were supposed to represent was near impossible, and so led to confusion and a lack of communication and understanding on both sides. A lot of the problem was that the counter-culture generation knew *instinctively* that the rules and structures of the societies of mankind were malignant and destructive, but lacked the conceptual tools to understand *why*.

Society is a construction of many levels of both surface and profound *beliefs* that collectively make up what I call a *social mythology*. Every society has a mythology comprised of thousands of interlocking and self-supporting myths, many of which the members of the society accept as *facts*. Some of these myths are so *universally accepted* and intractable that most of the population doesn't even realize their presence, though these beliefs guide their every motion and action.

Reality is the set of conditions that *truly exist in the world*, regardless of our willingness to accept them. These conditions outline the *structure of creation*, and are *easily observable* since they govern every aspect of our existence.

W hen the social mythology is not laid out according to the principles that actually govern creation, then that society cannot help but be ineffective on a personal, species, and world level. If that society is founded on myths that not only *ignore* but actually *vilify* the true structure of reality, then that society quickly becomes not only ineffective, but *destructive* to itself, its constituents, and the entire planet.

This is the difference between reality and our social mythology and is the simple root of virtually all of our ills, be they physical, mental, emotional, spiritual, or community. Our society not only ignores the true structure of reality, it *abhors* it. Our mythology runs completely *counter* to the way the universe is actually constructed, so much so that we must turn a blind eye to the evidence we encounter every second of our lives, evidence that is neither confusing or mysterious but is in fact completely *blatant* and *undeniable*. If we did not ignore it, this evidence would crash down upon our mythology and quite probably destroy our lives, because we would be completely unable to accept it.

But accept it we must. Mankind, as a species, is on the whole an *ineffective* and *destructive* influence, and must undergo a profound change in his mythology, bringing it in line with the principles of reality, or he will never be able to live harmoniously with himself and the universe around him.

But of the Tree of Knowledge of good and evil, thou shalt not eat of it: for in the day that thou eatest thereof, thou shalt surely die.

*— **Genesis** 2:17*

The dust of exploded beliefs may make a fine sunset.

— Geoffrey Madan, 1895-1947

It is undesirable to believe a proposition when there is no ground whatever for supposing it true.

— Bertrand Russell, 1872-1970

KNOWLEDGE: SOCIETY'S DNA

Just as a cell perpetuates itself with information-laden DNA, society perpetuates itself with information-laden "knowledge." We are all programmed with information that is designed to keep the *organism of society* alive and functioning, so we may each fulfill our part. Just like cancer cells reprogramming healthy cells, though, this social programming completely covers up our true, reality-based programming, and makes us over into ineffective, destructive beings from our very *birth*.

The only way to shed this malignant programming is by conceptually understanding that it is not inherently *true* or *superior* or even *accurate*. As individuals, we are in awe of the sophistication of our "knowledge" as a society, and obediently go about fulfilling our social programming, never allowing an obvious *reality* to give us pause: *every society, no matter how backward or advanced, considers its "knowledge" superior.*

In a hundred years, our "knowledge" will be laughed at just as we dismiss the beliefs of eighteenth or nineteenth century societies. In two hundred years, our most profound "truths" will be considered folklore and faery tales. We don't want to accept this, because it points out that this kind of "knowledge" is not true *knowledge* at all, just subjective, *mythic* information. Its only purpose is to program each of us away from our *designed purpose* and into *society's* fold, perpetuating and strengthening itself.

The sophistication of this mythic programming is surpassed only by its sheer volume. Trying to dismantle it, piece by piece, is like trying to eradicate a ten-story building brick by brick. It would be tremendously difficult at best, if not impossible. The only alternative is *destroying it completely in one swift act*, accepting that our entire personal belief system is based on inaccurate, destructive myths and must be replaced.

Must it be an act of faith? No, because we have the ability, more or less, to suspend our beliefs, walk outside the building, and look it over objectively to see if it is founded on *reality* or if it completely ignores the obvious construction of the universe. From within we can see nothing.

Suspension of our beliefs is very difficult, because it is hard to recognize just how deep and intractable those beliefs are. However, suspending them as best we can, we can look over the *principles of reality* as objectively as possible and easily see, because of their inescapable, blatant nature, that the building *must come down*.

It's not just what we inherit from our mothers and fathers that haunts us. It's all kinds of old defunct beliefs, and things like that. It's not that they actually live on us; they are simply lodged there, and we cannot get rid of them.

— **Henrik Ibsen, 1828-1906**

It all depends on how we look at things, and not on how they are in themselves.

— **Carl Jung**

ALL KNOWLEDGE IS BELIEF

No two people completely agree on *anything*, no matter their education or background. Whether the topic is religion between two priests or physics between eminent scientists, no two will completely agree. No matter how sophisticated we become, the universe never offers any non-interpretive results, any conclusive *facts*, for the simple reason that we all interpret the world individually, because of our individual viewpoints. And we each consider our beliefs to be *facts*.

How'd you come by your beliefs? Would you have them if you were born a Bedouin? A Buddhist? An Aborigine? No. Your beliefs are usually quite similar to the beliefs of those around you. Not exactly, but close.

Everything you know and accept as fact, as well as the things you classify as beliefs, are simply your beliefs. It matters little if ten thousand or ten million or the entire world agrees with you; truth cannot be voted in by majority, or even by unanimous declaration. You have absolutely no assurance that the things you hold as true are anything more than deceptions and misconceptions.

Oh, we all *feel* we know the truth, what is right and wrong. We all know that, by and large, we're doing all right.

That we're doing a good job, raising our kids the best we know how, being responsible adults, living constructive, enjoyable lives.

The above paragraph could include anyone on the planet — from insane religious dictators to the quiet family next door, from Zulu warriors to hookers to deacons to psychos to televangelists. What we're really doing is *living up to the standards of our personal mythology.* Our so-called "knowledge" has guided us to become prisoners of our own construction of personal myths.

Here is an example, from my own life, of how my *inner desire* to be an artist interacted with the *social mythology* (in the form of my parents' belief systems) to create some "truisms" that guided many of my decisions and actions:

"Well, the detail is great, but your anatomy is all wrong."

I smiled, trying to extract a compliment out of my dad's statement. "Yeah. Looks pretty good, doesn't it?"

He was a young, good-looking fifty-two, curly hair, glasses. He examined my pen and ink rendering again, the ultimate work of a teenage artist.

"Well, I wish I could do that fine detailed work. But Bill, you need to get some schooling if you ever want to make any money at this. It's amateurish. You'll never make a living at it."

I looked at the drawing again. It was a man in armor entering a bar, a sword and sorcery scene I'd spent hours on.

"How do you like it, Mom?"

She tilted her head back to use the bottom of her bifocals. "Well, it's pretty. What is it?"

I guess I should have been hurt, and maybe I was, deep down inside. "A knight going into a bar."

"Oh, yes. I see now. Why don't you do some windmills or horses? You know, people around here buy those western scenes."

I must have had this conversation with my parents dozens of times, in one form or another, on one subject or another. It took me years to understand some of the complex and subtle personal mythology I created out of these situations:

1. There's no reason to invest a lot of time in doing artwork unless you can reasonably expect to make money at it.

2. You can't succeed without the proper education.

3. There is an actual *distinction* between an amateur and a professional and the difference is *obvious*.

4. Creativity can and should be manipulated to meet market needs and society's standards.

And so on. Oh, they are very *reasonable* beliefs. Many would call all or some of them *facts*. Problem is, they just don't hold up when you look at the world. Many people succeed without a "proper" education. There is no real distinction between amateurs and professionals. And true creativity often cannot conform to social standards.

This is an example of how we accept social programming as fact, when the observational evidence just does not support it. We alter our perception of the world to keep this information true. Here are some more examples of social myths that cannot be supported by observational evidence:

We should strive to be productive members of society.

We should strive to achieve as much security as possible for ourselves and our family.

We have the ability to affect the universe the way we want.

Certain situations are inherently better than others.

Certain values are inherently better than others.

The list goes on and on. You look at some of those beliefs listed above and you immediately feel they cannot be anything but true, they are so deep and universally accepted. The fact is, though, that there is *absolutely no empirical, objective evidence that supports any of the above beliefs*, or that adherence to them generates any consistently positive effect.

Does a loving family produce a well-balanced child any more often than it produces a misfit? Or a genius? Or a sociopath? Does poverty prevent positive growth or propel an individual toward greatness? Does wealth and security offer the groundwork for aiding the less fortunate, or do the rich lapse into a self-centered, self-indulgent existence?

The truth is, one situation is not better or worse than another. Lack of security may prepare a youth for misfortune and better advise him if he comes into wealth; or it may render him incapable of making decisions in a world he or she knows to be capricious.

Also, does teaching our children to be honest and moral make them suckers for the real world? It did me. It took me years to understand that people lied — simply because I was raised to be honest, by honest people. I can assure you, this is not an advisable curriculum if you want to prepare a child for the real world. It brings a lot of pain and confusion.

To keep our personal mythology intact, though, we remove this conflicting information into a mental room marked "aberrant" or "exceptions." My own dad retired from an artwork job with no formal education, but he didn't want me to believe that this could realistically be done. Through countless information-sharing events like this, society propagates its mythology. Even if one person's experience has proven the information to be inaccurate, the indoctrination continues because the individual doesn't want to pass along socially unacceptable information.

If something is true, how can there be an exception, as in the case of my needing an education to be able to succeed? Is there an exception to gravity? To inertia? The fact is, we *want* these beliefs to be true, we accept them as *generally* true so we can get on with the business of our lives. *We accept them as approximate truths,* because we have nothing else, nothing more accurate to replace them with. And so society continually re-establishes its mythic programming, generation after generation.

We are born with genetic predispositions into a certain environment. Our social programming begins *immediately,* if not even while we are still in the womb. Society itself is formed when a number of individuals with similar enough beliefs come together. Since those individuals are generally genetically predisposed to fit in with that society anyway, they are readily suited for the social programming, strengthening the mythology of the society as a whole. The larger and more uniform a society becomes, the more intractable the most common beliefs become. Certain approximate truths become facts, simply because they are so widely held.

As a society grows, it becomes varied, with each sub-society following the path described above, likely still having much in common with the larger society, but perhaps differing in a few significant areas. Over time, certain beliefs may become so intractable and accepted that their presence is invisible — they become accepted as *universal* or *common* or *self-evident truths.*

We should accept nothing as factual or true; belief is a construction of approximate truths, common truths, and myths, based on genetic predisposition and environmental/ social conditioning.

How can we possibly say that *all* our knowledge is really belief, based on false myth and inaccurate approximate truths? The evidence is all around us. Science has "proven" that our universe is 99.9% empty space. That subatomic features are indeterminate until consciously *observed*. That bacteria are constantly in our body and remain dormant until our immune system is impaired. How long ago did we "know" that the universe was made up of solid matter? That the proton, neutron, and electron were mechanical bits of matter and energy? That the human body was fine until attacked from the outside?

How long ago did we "know" that women were inferior to men and should not be allowed to vote? That mental disorders were not physically treatable? That sickness was the wrath of God? That the Earth was the center of the universe? That man could never run a four-minute mile? That the planet was only a few thousand years old?

Oh, it's not arrogance that leads us to believe that our approximate truths are much more substantial than those of our ancestors or neighbors; we believe our myths for the same reason they believed theirs — to stay sane. To protect ourselves and our society. And our descendants will think us just as foolish, and themselves every bit as superior.

It's easy to see that our "knowledge" is just a collection of very sophisticated myths, just by looking at the examples above. There are hundreds of examples easily observable every day. How can any of us be so arrogant as to assume our personal "knowledge" has any value or substance *whatsoever* when we are the only creature on the entire planet with that particular set of beliefs? Only by filing all the contradictory information away, out of our sight, can we escape the fact that "knowledge" is like a snowflake pattern; not true or false, just one pattern out of millions to choose from. Some are simple, some complex, but all are essentially the same: *they all are individual expressions of the **conditions** that created them.*

Accepting the *conditions*, or true structure of reality, is like simply accepting the ramifications of *gravity*. The observable effects of gravity are incorporated into our every action and thought. *Knowledge* is any individual's attempt to define exactly *what* gravity *is*. Gravity is the condition that must be accepted in order to live effectively. If our knowledge, or mythic information/social programming, does not accurately follow the *observable structure of gravity*, then we are in for a world of hurt, and will continue to be as long as we *ignore* the obvious structure and effects of gravity.

This example explains why mankind is having such trouble. Our *knowledge* is not in line with reality, and so we face obstacles and difficulties every day, every minute. Only if we excise this unneeded, useless, overwhelming mountain of mythic information can we see the structure, the *principles of reality* that govern our existence, and begin living effectively, harmoniously.

The first principle, that all our "knowledge" is simply mythic social programming, is readily evidenced in everyday life. The deepest investigations into the nature of our physical universe corroborate this truth; scientists have found that *exactly pinpointing* the physical characteristics of the foundation "particles" is impossible. Subatomic particles cannot even be defined as either *waves* or *particles*, since under different circumstances they display varying characteristics.

How much more *profound* and *obvious* can a basic structure of reality be? How can "knowledge" be *anything* other than useless, mythic information when the very *physical characteristics of the universe are determined by the observer*, and can and *do* display self-contradicting behaviors, depending upon the characteristics of the observer?

You don't have to dig that deep to understand that knowledge is belief. The mere fact that *what we expect to happen* in the world around us so rarely, in fact, happens should be enough to convince us that our information is, at best, inaccurate. Do we *know* how to raise kids? How to find happiness? How to find security? What the stock market will do? What love is? What those around us think of us? What certain "safe" chemicals might do to us ten years down the road? Who will get cancer, who won't? What exact color "red" is? What is honorable, what is ethical? We ourselves shift our own knowledge around to make room for that which we desire to be true.

For example, at one time I hired on at a local grocery store as a floor clerk and as store artist. I searched the job out and took it because it presented itself and I needed an income, but also because I was learning a great deal about myself and my inner motives at the time. The universe brought to me exactly what I requested at the time.

At the job, I made a good friend who wanted to hear a lot of what I had to say about life, since he was going through a difficult time and was having trouble dealing with it. Everyone there was impressed with my hard work and bright attitude.

However, as time went on, I realized that I had to leave the job, because no matter how I changed the position around, I couldn't make myself continue to enjoy it. So I left. At the time, even I didn't understand all the reasons behind my having to leave.

But those still working at the store, faced with a hard-working, upbeat individual who left a job they remained at, had to perceive the event in a way that didn't threaten their own view of life. One "knew" I quit because I didn't want to pay my child support. Another "knew" I quit because I wanted to do artwork and not the regular store stocking. Still others "knew" it was because I didn't like my supervisor.

Their memory of my time at the store was altered to accommodate this new, necessary perception. Quickly I became a poor worker, an "o.k." artist, had a bad attitude, wanted everything "my" way, or had been influenced by my new friend, who had a "bad attitude." They all had to redefine who I was and what happened in order to fit their perception of reality and not threaten their program of self-worth. They stay in unfulfilling, frustrating jobs (from their account) in order to meet societal and financial obligations and responsibilities (and to fulfill the standard 40 hr-week and advancement-oriented philosophy of our culture), and by doing so they define themselves as "good" people. So, by taking an action that violated their personal belief system and program of self-worth, I had to be completely reclassified in their minds to support their existing view of life. I had to be a "bad" person. It would be virtually impossible for them to understand the reasons I took the job, that working hard is just part of who I am, and that I just "felt" it was time to go. None of that could possibly fit their view of life and people, so they couldn't accept it, however I answered their questions.

In other words, the *structure of reality* is that the universe is entirely *subjective to the individual. Knowledge* is simply arbitrary mythic information society uses to program its population in order to perpetuate itself. This programming hides reality from us by twisting our observations around to fit its own view of the principles and structure of creation. As a result, we become further and further out of sync with reality, having to redefine, re-interpret, and edit more of our own memories to accommodate society's false view of creation.

A society that demands conformity and promotes a certain set of values, ethics, and morals is in direct contradiction to the structure of reality, where all such ideas are completely individual. Our society does not accept this; it not only attempts to program a certain set of beliefs into every individual (thereby *already* contradicting reality), the very myths it attempts to program us with are in direct conflict with the other obvious facets of reality.

Security is mortals' chiefest enemy.

— **Shakespeare,** *Macbeth*

Term, holidays, term, holidays, till we leave school, and then work, work, work till we die.

— **C.S. Lewis, 1898-1963**

I slept, and dreamed that life was Beauty; I woke, and found that life was Duty.

— **Ellen Sturgis Hooper, 1816-1841**

SECURITY AND RESPONSIBILITY: SOCIETY'S CARROT AND WHIP

Accepting that all *knowledge* is simply mythic information is simply a matter of observing the world objectively — every viewpoint can be substantiated through so-called *evidence*, even views which are exactly opposite. It just depends on what evidence we deem pertinent — we *decide* what information is related to the situation, then gather the supporting documentation. No matter how deeply you examine an issue or an object, it can be infinitely fractured down into a multitude of conflicting data. Even breaking an object down to its sub-atomic structure gives us no "deciding," objective answer — subatomic phenomena act in an entirely self-conflicting manner, as waves or as particles, *depending only upon how the phenomena are observed.* In effect, that which observes *decides* what structure the evidence is going to support.

Knowledge is the programming tool of society through which it defines the world and our place in it. "Defines" is the key word here, because any definition is simply taking an arbitrary viewpoint. Evidence can be gathered to support any perspective, but society wants to endorse only that which perpetuates its existence and superiority.

Two categories by which society maintains deep, profound control over our lives are the mythic concepts of *security* and *responsibility*. These are the twin pillars of our cultural order from which virtually all motivation and action spring. The way in which society defines these concepts to us lies in *direct conflict* with the true form and process of creation.

A letter comes with instructions to report for jury duty. You view it as a responsibility and go, easily finding the defendant not guilty, due to reasonable doubt. The next week he rapes and kills a local high school cheerleader, admitting freely to having committed many such crimes. You start waking up in the middle of the night to the sound of your windshield being broken or a threatening voice on the phone, and your kids are ostracized or worse at school. The neighbors, once your good friends, no longer even look in your direction.

The insurance premium comes due and you pay, knowing full well it's your responsibility to protect your family. A call comes from the police that your son was involved in an accident and has lost both of his arms. State of the art prosthetic limbs and the required therapy to use them are not, you are informed, covered by your policy. A lawsuit would cost as much as the prosthetic limbs themselves.

To afford the kids' braces and the roofing job your house so desperately needs, you take on a second job. Eight weeks later you fall seriously ill, the doctor saying you have been under too much physical and mental stress, and your blood pressure is way too high. Six weeks after that you have a nervous breakdown, and your wife divorces you and takes the kids. "But I was doing it for you," you cry weakly.

We are born with a certain genetic code into a certain environment. The world is a near-infinite cauldron of interdependent, interactive motion, action, and reaction, that has been going on long before any of us came into the world and will continue long after man disappears from the scene. An infinite number of events shaped the world and brought it to its present state, and an infinite variety of both microscopic and macroscopic events take place every minute to propel the world toward its unknown destiny.

That infinite cauldron of action designed and created us to fulfill an exact, precise need; just as every flower, every bee, and every ray of light fulfills a purpose that is necessary to the whole. In the natural world, this true responsibility is carried out automatically; with man, his true purpose is covered and restricted by social rules and programming. Society demands we fulfill its agenda and ignore or at least restrict our inner desires. These inner needs are even *vilified* by many parts of our culture.

Society would have us believe that, as individual specks in the midst of all of this, we can somehow be held *accountable* if we do not fulfill its definition of our responsibilities. If we are jobless, it is our fault. If we are alcoholics, it is our fault. If our kids grow up to be criminals, it is our fault. There is no such thing as an "accident" — it is, of course, always someone's fault, someone's responsibility.

We all do what we have to do, based on our genetic code, our environment, and our individual desires. All our actions are the sum of those conditions, none of which we had anything to do with creating. We are without responsibility — we didn't create the conditions, and we have no idea what the immediate or eventual ramifications of our actions will be — positive or negative, good or bad. We are under no obligation of any sort to try to live up to the criteria of society — because society cannot guarantee our success, our security, or our happiness.

The burden of this false responsibility is immense. We are consumed with guilt, self-doubt, anxiety, and stress. We calculate every move, as if we could predict the outcome. We worry about every decision, every expense, every action lest we be judged irresponsible by the community and ostracized or thrown into jail. Because we want to be able to blame others for events beyond anyone's real control, we must first toe the line of accountability ourselves. Then we can feel comfortable in reproaching those who have "failed" to live up to their responsibilities, when the unforeseen happens.

"That could never happen to me," we whisper to ourselves when we see the homeless, the diseased, the victims of a tragic accident, or those on trial. "I live up to my responsibilities."

We try to live up to the program of responsibilities because we are promised security if we do. We subscribe to this because we desperately want security to be something real and attainable. We blind ourselves to the inequities, the corruption, the lies, the waste, and the oppression of our social order because, if we don't, then we can kiss the holy grail of personal security goodbye. Suddenly we're malcontents, we're irresponsible, we're criminals that threaten everyone's security — or at least the belief that such security really exists.

Security is an illusory reward, a carrot used to attract us into society-fulfilling action. *Responsibility* is a whip, a threat used to drive us, or intimidate us into similar activity. Both are phantom concepts that can be interpreted and re-defined an infinite number of ways, only dependent upon our personal point of view. We interpret our goals and motivations according to our society-programmed belief system, which determines how we view the evidence and which evidence is pertinent to the situation. It's virtually fool-proof; society not only programs your *objectives*, it programs how you collect and evaluate the *evidence of your observations* to support the desirability of those goals and your progress in attaining them.

For us, there is only the trying, the rest is not our business.

   — **T.S. Eliot, 1888-1965**

What we anticipate seldom occurs; what we least expected generally happens.

   — **Benjamin Disraeli, 1804-1881**

For want of a nail, the shoe was lost; for want of a shoe, the horse was lost;

For want of a horse, the rider was lost; for want of a rider, the battle was lost;

For want of a battle, the kingdom was lost!

   — **George Herbert, 1593-1633**

ALL THINGS ARE IMPERMANENT, ALL RAMIFICATIONS UNKNOWN

We have used honest examination of the universe to understand that all "knowledge" is simply what we choose to believe; we can use the same simple technique to dismiss our false notions of *responsibility* and *security*.

By honestly observing creation, we can easily see that all things are impermanent. Everything is subject to the blatant, undeniable processes of *birth, change, death, and rebirth*. Everything is born into existence, is effective for a certain time, changes, and then dies, *giving birth to the new*. The cyclic dynamic of birth, change, death, and rebirth, throughout every scale and location, is the fundamental process that both unites and guides every aspect of creation. The universe itself is thought in many quarters to undergo cyclic birth, expansion and change, collapse, and rebirth. Certainly all that resides within this universe adheres unceasingly to this program.

Early in the life of the universe, all forces were united; the death of this unity was the birth of the cosmos. From a primordial cosmic "soup" of fermions and quarks, atomic particles were born; these atomic particles eventually formed chemical elements that later united en masse and formed the first generation of stars in the black void.

Birth, change, death, rebirth. The death of the Unified Field Era ushered in the Inflation Era, which succumbed to the Electroweak Era. Each Era had its characteristic dominant and submissive traits that defined its beginning and end. Certain characteristics could only be effective for a certain duration of time in a certain environment. Over a given period of time, with a change in the environment, one system of organization fell to a hardier, more effective system. As we now measure time, these Eras lasted about .00000000000000000000000000000000001 of a second.

The first generation of lonely stars, with no family of planets, were of the Population III Era. These pioneering entities used their nuclear furnaces to transform huge amounts of hydrogen and helium into heavier elements, then died in explosions that heaved these heavier elements into the void, seeding it with the matter we all owe our existence to. We are of the Population I Era, the generation of familial solar systems. Within the Population I Era, Earth was born and will die. Then the Population 0 Era, or whatever its residents may choose to term it, will eventually begin.

On a shorter scale of time, the history of the Earth mirrors the same principles of creation that guide and shape the Universe. Through many Earthly eras we have developed from a primordial "soup" very similar to the sub-atomic soup of the infant universe, to the current state of ecological structure. Each era had its characteristic strengths and frailties, which transformed the environment and gave rise to the next era — from organic compounds to single cells to groups of cells and on to the very complex, interdependent systems we see today.

Birth, change, death, and rebirth. A system rises, transforms itself and the world, then dies, as the transformed world can no longer support it. Then there is the rebirth of the new, hardier, more efficient system, better equipped to proliferate in the new world, from the ashes of the old.

Within the written history of mankind and his societies we can see this dynamic in action. Though it occurs on a smaller scale in physical size, and a shorter duration in time, the course of human history follows the explicit rule of Creation; birth, change, death, and rebirth. Because this divine law operates regardless of *dimension* (size, time), it is certainly in effect at the level of the individual on a day to day, moment by moment basis. If the fundamental physical laws and characteristics of the entire universe could change many times in 10^{-35} of a second, when its size inflated from a point to a basketball, then profound change and action is not limited to large scales and time frames.

Think of the billions of cells that make up each of us, and the unimaginable cycle of birth, death, change, and rebirth going on every second within our own bodies. Then go on to the chemical and subatomic regeneration and change going on every billionth of a second. At that scale, an hour of the day is the lifetime of an entire world, the lifetime of each individual is an Era. Our size, from that perspective, is that of the Universe.

All entities in the universe follow this rule of *system re-organization*. Nothing is not subject to it. Living organisms, inanimate objects, societies, ideas, beliefs — they all follow the guiding pattern of birth, death, change, and rebirth.

Accepting reality means dismissing our concept of finding "security" in the world — it cannot exist, is not meant to exist, because creation is designed to *continually reorganize into new, effective, harmonious manifestations*. We perceive only a minute fraction of the universe around us, of the infinite, interlocking, interdependent chain of events that stretches out through every direction and dimension. The idea that we can chisel a secure position out of this ever-changing, dynamic universe, or that we are *responsible* for achieving certain situations, or for the ramifications of our actions, is without any possible merit. The concepts are in direct contradiction with observable reality, the process of birth, change, death, and rebirth, and our own pathetically limited perception of the infinite universe.

There are periods of time when all goes well, when we perceive ourselves as safe and secure, when living up to our responsibilities provides us with satisfaction and fulfillment of our desires. But it is an equally observable fact that these periods are always *temporary*, subject to birth, change, and death. The flow of life is *evident*. The only way to subscribe to the concept of "security" is to blind yourself to large portions of creation.

The same is true of *responsibility*. How often do our actions have the ramifications that we desire? How often do unforeseen, unexpected events crash into our lives? The fact is, anything can happen to us at any time — it is only our refusal to admit this, to admit how little we know, how little we understand, how little we perceive of the universe that allows us to think we can be held personally responsible for anything at all. "Personal responsibility," as defined by society, is the height of arrogance — and of ignorance. It assumes we have a near complete understanding of the form and processes of creation, near enough to be held accountable for our actions.

We don't even understand *ourselves*, why we do what we do, what motivates our actions, much less the physical, mental, and spiritual forces that guide the universe around us. We don't understand the quantum mechanics that are the basic principles of the physical realm; we don't understand the physiological processes that govern our mental arrangement; we don't even know what generates thought — yet we are supposed to be responsible for our actions? In planning our activities, we have absolutely no idea what forces or situations will arise — because every day brings an infinite array of possibilities.

The idea of responsibility is an obvious farce — it and "security," as socially defined currently, *simply cannot exist in creation*. Accepting this is merely an act of allowing what is obvious in the universe past our mental barriers, without re-interpretation and corruption by our belief system. This all-consuming quest for security and the burden of responsibility is at the heart of much of man's physical, mental, and spiritual difficulties, because it is not in line with the structure of the universe he lives in.

Our true responsibility lies in fulfilling our original designed purpose, *not* the obviously ineffective and destructive programming of society. Just as a cell, or ant, or a bee fulfills an inherent purpose without regard for the so-called ramifications, so too must man learn to do the same.

True security, then, lies in freely and honestly expressing your inherent purpose in creation, without regard for the socially defined "consequences," which we easily see cannot, in any way, be predicted.

They are good, they are bad, they are weak, they are strong, They are wise, they are foolish — so am I.
   — **Sam Walters Foss**

Resolve to be thyself; and know that who finds himself, loses his misery.
   — **Matthew Arnold, 1822-1888**

There's a sucker born every minute.
   — **Phineas T. Barnum, 1810-1891**

EGO:
SOCIETY'S BLINDERS

There is a distinction between *individuality* and *ego*; individuality is the expression of our inherent desire, while ego is the *belief* that there are separate, distinct *divisions* between objects in time and space, and that such objects (including non-physical objects such as thoughts, concepts, motivations, etc.) can be *evaluated* according to its belief system. Ego is why we look at ourselves as separate beings, living in a particular time and place with a certain set of ideas. We look at other people as something completely separate and distinct from ourselves, as we do other countries, other religions, other planets, etc. Ego is a divisive, categorization process that allows us to separate one *thing*, or *event* from another and classify each according to our perspective.

Without *ego*, society could never program the concepts of *security* and *responsibility* into us, simply because we wouldn't be able to view ourselves as distinct, separate entities in need of any so-called "security" or capable of personal "responsibility."

Ego is what allows each of us to act in a self-serving manner, heedless of a reality that plainly states that all our actions are completely *indefinite* — we *think* we are building some sort of security, because our *ego* views these things we collect for our "security" as distinct items that are now *ours* or that now serve *our* needs, evaluating each according to the security program. The simple truth is, all things in this reality are here as the result of an infinitely complex chain of events, and have their own *inherent purpose* to fulfill — they can no more be "ours" than a quarter in your pocket "belongs" to your *spleen*. The two are roughly equal constituents in reality, just as bone tissue and nerve tissue are roughly equal parts of our body — *they each have a purpose to fulfill*, and should be able to move freely from one purpose to the next.

An interesting point here is: with what do we evaluate our evaluation process? Most of us simply go about collecting security and fulfilling our responsibilities, sending each item or situation up to the evaluation center for examination, then act on the forthcoming verdict, *never pausing to question the evaluation process itself*. Where did it come from? How was it formed? Is it really providing me with happiness and fulfillment? Can its decisions be validated through objective observation, or must the evidence be re-interpreted to support the evaluation center's selections?

Our evaluation process itself ignores many obvious facets of life and reality in its judgments. It is a mechanism that defines the choices, chooses according to its existing program, and then interprets the result to support its choice. It is limited by the dualistic concepts of good and evil, right and wrong, positive and negative, and doesn't take into account that these concepts, like everything else in creation, are *relative to the interpretation of the observer*. To justify our actions, we must classify those that behave differently as "wrong" or "evil" or "negative," thereby salvaging our own self-worth. Only by *transcending* our existence within our personal evaluation centers can we move beyond the limiting, conflicting, destructive arena of judgement, guilt, blame, and justification.

Love your enemies, do good to them which hate you.

— ***Luke*** 6:27

Our body is a machine for living. It is organized for that, it is its nature. Let life go on in it unhindered and let it defend itself, it will do more than if you paralyse it by encumbering it with remedies.

— **Leo Tolstoy, *War and Peace***

In science as in life, it is well known that a chain of events can have a point of crisis that could magnify small changes.

— **James Gleick, *Chaos***

ALL THINGS ARE PART OF THE WHOLE

All things in reality are connected to each other like a giant *multi-dimensional jigsaw puzzle*, not only inter-locked through space, but also through time, as well as perhaps other dimensions. Our ego has been trained by society to ignore this and try to construct its own, self-con-tained puzzle for our own security, to fulfill our personal responsibilities. When we do this, we mentally block out the obvious *inadequacies* of our construction *and* the *harm* we are doing to the *whole*.

The distinction between our *selves* and the "outside world" is another inaccurate piece of mythic information that does not allow us to have a proper mental model of reality. Just as our skin "lives" on our muscular structure, there is another layer of life that "lives" on our skin, every bit as real and solid as any of our internal systems. It is the atmosphere.

Not only is the atmosphere of the world present all over the surface of our bodies, it is also throughout our *lungs* and *circulatory* system. It is teeming with vital chemicals we could not exist without, as well as with microbes and bacteria and other organisms — just as all our internal systems are. It is a system that is fully integral to our survival.

There is no real dividing line between our bodies and the rest of the world, just as there is no real dividing line between our different "internal" systems. We *could* view the circulatory system as separate from the other systems, but in reality it is totally hooked up to and integrated with every other part of our body, *as well as the "external" atmosphere system.*

An individual cell can be taken from our body and examined. It is a living organism, complete in itself and will live for quite a while completely separate from us without any aid — quite longer than we ourselves would live if removed from the body of the Earth and its atmosphere.

Can a single cell see itself as a being that ends at its cell wall? Can a whole *organ*, say the heart, see itself as an independent creature that ends at its surface, or at the surface of its extensions, the *veins* and *arteries*? Can a human see itself as a creature that ends at its skin? Drawing a line there is totally arbitrary; there is no evidence that we, as an organism, end at the skin. In fact, the evidence is that we do not. The *observational evidence* is that the organism continues on, from the smallest part of the individual cell on out, extending infinitely outward. The world itself could not "live" if removed from a certain distance from the sun, and the sun itself is an obedient member of the galactic community of stars, et cetera, ad infinitum.

Again, we see that no matter how sophisticated our "knowledge" becomes, what time in history we live, many of us continue to ignore the structure of reality. Everything in reality belongs to a system of birth, change, death, and rebirth, or a living *organism*. We try to categorize things into classifications of organic or inorganic material, intelligent or unintelligent species, even as far as beings with or without *souls*.

This obsession with *categorization* is part of society's mythic information program, which falls apart with only a little objective observation. What is inorganic, and what is organic? If calcium, zinc, and iron are inorganic minerals, what are they when they are inside our bodies? Our entire body is constructed of *inorganic materials,* so what makes them organic? Is it because the entire *system* is "alive?" Isn't this also true of the entire planet? Or a single cell? Or the entire Universe?

We classify ourselves *above* other animals because of our so-called *intelligence.* Why? If we instead chose to classify species according to effectiveness on the planet, mankind would be at the bottom of the totem pole. If we classify according to *beauty,* or *grace,* or *sheer numbers,* mankind wouldn't make the top third of any category. The fact is that our *intelligence,* as we now use it, makes us a *cancer* in the world organism, thereby condemning us to the bottom of the ladder of life-forms.

If the religious concept of a "soul" is used to grant us superior status, then this leaves us begging for many explanations. Do Siamese twins have one, or two souls? When does a soul "enter" the body? Does it inhabit every cell, every strand of hair? Does it inhabit the completely separate and self-sustaining microbes, bacteria, and viruses that live with us in our body? Does it inhabit those born with no brain activity? Those in a coma for years? Just humans, or other species? What about aliens, beings not from our world? How would we determine whether or not *they* have "souls?"

I am not saying that there is no such thing as a "soul." As a matter of fact, the observable evidence *demands* that there be a part of us that makes us distinct. Once again, though, society has corrupted reality for its own ends and has deceived us into misunderstanding what a "soul" really is.

Though we are all part of the whole, each part, no matter how large or minuscule, has an individual designed purpose that *serves the designed purpose of the entire entity.* This *individual dynamic* is completely harmonious with the form and processes of reality, if it is allowed to interact honestly, without interpretation or restriction.

At the bottom end (currently) of our observational spectrum are individual *leptons, quarks,* and *bosons,* which make up sub-atomic matter and carry the forces which bind them together. As far as science knows, *all matter and energy* are made up of these entities. Do they have "souls?" Are they "alive?" What they *do* have are individual dynamics that guide them in fulfilling their inherent purpose in creation.

These entities (I cannot really call them *particles*, because they are not true particles at all) position themselves together into *systems* that are born, change, die, and are reborn. Two of these systems are called *protons* and *neutrons*.

These two systems combine with each other and other "particles systems" to form *atoms*, which also are born, change, die, and are reborn. Carbon atoms, for example, clump together in a wild variety of forms, some of which group together to form the basic structures of what we commonly call *organic* compounds and molecules. When these molecules and compounds integrate into systems a certain way, they form *DNA*, or the chemical structure inherent in all "organic life." Within a single cell in your body (and your body contains *billions* of individual cells), there are thousands of structures that are built within the cell and sent out to other cells, structures that clean, process, receive, encode, and *create*.

All these entities are born, change, die, and are reborn, in the form of new cells. Just as there are countless leptons, quarks, and bosons making up self-sufficient structures that form a single *molecule*, there are countless molecular constructions that make up a single *cell*, and then countless cells that make up a single *organic system* (eyes, heart, liver, muscles). Put enough of those organic systems together and you have a man, or a dolphin, or an ant, or a whale. Put enough like individuals together and you have a *species*, then an *ecological system*, a planet, a solar system, a galaxy, a *universe.*

Can life exist on so grand a scale? Does an organism that stretches the distance between stars seem unreal? Impossible? How can an organic entity encompass so much empty space?

How does life span the huge gaps of empty space between the nucleus of an atom to its electron, and then on to the next atom? The distance between sun and planets is no greater *proportionately* than that between nucleus and electrons, and the space between no emptier. Atoms are actually comprised of over *99% empty space.* If protons, neutrons, and electrons were like suns and planets, then a being on one of those planets would look at the human body as something just as large and empty and devoid of life as we now see the universe.

We view ourselves as some sort of solid, individual whole, because of society's programming, and refuse to look at *reality* that plainly demonstrates that the universe is a *whole*, which is basically the same regardless of *scale* or *point of reference.* Whether you look at the universe from the position of an atomic particle, a cell, a human, a planet, or a galaxy, you will see yourself as an *individual entity*, a member of the *hierarchy of interconnected, interdependent systems*, comprised of infinite sub-systems and a part of infinite "greater" systems, whether physical, mental, or spiritual.

Ego is the structure of our personal mythology. It is *who* and *what* we believe ourselves to be in creation. Individuality is the design of our inner dynamic. If our ego is constructed to give our individual dynamic the opportunity to express itself freely in the world, we are happy and fulfilled. However, if the ego is constructed in a way that prohibits, alters, or restricts our individuality, we run into trouble. The prevalent social mythology, which programs much of our ego, attempts to define life in very strict terms that are increasingly out of touch with reality. As creation flows and moves toward a more effective social system, the old one tries to salvage or protect itself by creating even more restrictive barriers, laws, morals, ethics. As fewer and fewer individual dynamics can be expressed within the increasingly restrictive program of society as it seeks to protect itself from the "flow" of creation, the level of spiritual, mental, and physical imbalance and disharmony grows.

Our individual dynamic is currently chained to an ego that *restricts* and *modifies* its creative interaction with the universe, based upon an evaluation program that not only perceives an insignificant portion of the evidence upon which it makes its decisions, but also *reinterprets* the extremely limited portion of the results it *can* perceive *to support its original decision.*

The social mythology, which programs the ego, must allow the harmonious interaction of its component parts with creation to remain effective. This naturally means that *society must change* and accept its limitations, that it cannot define the relationship between the individual and creation or demand that relationship conform to certain "standards." Society cannot survive unless it understands its role in creation, *as an aid to the individual's relationship with creation,* and *not* as an entity meant to *define or interpret* the individual, creation, or the relationship between the two.

If society is deeply rooted in concepts and principles that are destructive and ineffective, and attempts to salvage itself through greater restrictions on the individual and his or her dynamic expression, that society is on a sure course toward complete breakdown and reorganization.

Discovering ways in which you are exceptional, the particular path you are meant to follow, is your business on this earth, whether you are afflicted or not.

— **Bernie Siegel, M.D., *Peace, Love, & Healing***

Where is the life we have lost in living?
Where is the wisdom we have lost in knowledge?
Where is the knowledge we have lost in information?

— **T.S. Eliot, 1888-1965**

TRIVIALIZATION: SOCIETY'S OPIATE

Our society has a habit of reducing its citizens to numbers, or statistics. Even though time and again we see the success achieved by single individuals, the overall subconscious message is that unless you achieve a certain level of financial worth, or fame, or power, your contribution to society and the world is negligible. By comparing your life with those in the media, you feel that you can accomplish little or that your life has less importance.

By instilling us with this attitude, our lives become "trivialized" by society. We are led to believe that our day-to-day actions have little impact in the overall scheme of things, and that we are only making it hard on ourselves if we run counter to the social program. We believe that we can only affect ourselves and those immediately surrounding us, so we concentrate on our own pleasures and successes — as defined by the social mythology.

This viewpoint of our lives being trivial in comparison to others and our actions and thoughts having little ramification outside of our personal lives is at the core of much of the frustration and anger in our society. In the modern world, we can't help but see ourselves as one human speck among billions, and can't help but evaluate our life in comparison to others that seem much more important. Many go insane because of the seeming absolute *banality* of the "average" person's mundane, daily existence.

In the previous chapter, we saw how we are all parts of the whole of creation, which is completely interconnected and interdependent. By understanding the *scale* and *position* structure of reality we can start to accept the true importance of every individual at any level of society, no matter their apparent — or *socially defined* — status in life.

One of the biggest obstacles facing those on the "quest" of spiritual enlightenment is that they feel limited, that their actions in the world have little or no effect. Many are tied to mundane, life-extinguishing jobs or careers that destroy spiritual motivation. Many are in surroundings that exhaust them physically and mentally, disabling them from walking the path of the quest.

Careers, family, obligations, social pressure, guilt, responsibilities — these are the modern-day *dragons* that mankind faces on his heroic path to transcendence. They are every bit as frightening and paralyzing as any monster that walked the earth, in fact or fantasy. The bravery that must be summoned to face these modern creatures easily eclipses that necessary to ride out against any oversized lizard — flaming breath or not. Who would dare to face the ogre of our own, self-imposed *responsibilities?* Who has the courage to stand against the kraken of *guilt*? Who has the conviction to fight against the army of *social pressure*?

If all mankind minus one, were of one opinion, and only one person were of the contrary opinion, mankind would be no more justified in silencing that one person, than he, if he had the power, would be justified in silencing mankind.

— **John Stuart Mill, 1806-1873**

Any man's death diminishes me, because I am involved in mankind. Therefore, never send to know for whom the bell tolls. It tolls for thee.

— **John Donne, 1571-1631**

ALL ENTITIES ARE EQUAL

Understanding the nature of *scale* and *position* gives us an invaluable tool when dealing with social trivialization, especially when one desires to bring spiritual transcendence into one's day to day life. *Scale* is the "size," or *arena of effectiveness*, of any system. For example, a city's scale encompasses its physical size, its population, and the duration of its existence, among other things. A person's *scale* is the combination of his or her presence in space and time and the effect they had during their stay.

Some cities, such as Rome, New York, Geneva, Berlin, Dodge City, and Auschwitz, exist on a higher level of symbolic meaning — their *scale* is larger. They are not mere cities, they have become representations of ideas, attitudes, or concepts that are beyond a city's normal range of *scales*. So too have many humans risen beyond the normal scale range and become symbolic of larger concepts or ideas.

Anything can transcend its normal scale into a higher symbolic meaning. Cadillac *means* excellence. Hiroshima *means* nuclear destruction. California *means* new ideas. Rolex *means* status and quality. Genghis Khan *means* barbaric tyranny.

However, these greater symbolic references are still only effective for a certain scale, which includes the range of time. When the symbolic meaning is no longer effective, it begins to die out, to be replaced with a new one more effective in the current scheme of creation.

A thing's place in this "scheme of creation" is referred to as its *position*. Not just its physical position, but its position as defined by all the pertinent aspects of its symbolic meaning — where it is, when it is, and what it is in the physical/mental/spiritual realm of creation. Everything has the qualities of position and scale, those qualities being completely *relative to the observer*. All scales and positions are equal to each other, because everything is made up of *infinite sub-systems* and is itself a part of *infinite systems*. Anything in creation is therefore both insignificant *and* all-important, depending upon the observer's own position and scale.

Your personal scale or position doesn't matter, because it reflects *every* scale and position — the qualities of creation are the same at any scale or position. No matter what level we "transcend" to, the structure and substance of creation will be the same and behave the same way, according to the fundamental principles that form and drive our existence.

Day to day physical life is a manifestation of the universal dynamic in action. It exists at a certain scale, with all the systems we encounter — physical, mental, spiritual — having certain positions and scales.

Every day we have the opportunity to fulfill our *designed purpose in our endeavors, and to allow ourselves to be re-created* as the universal dynamic sees fit, so that we remain effective (or increase our effective scale) in creation.

Realistically, it is hard to maintain a spiritual frame of mind in day to day life because we often view it as without any real spiritual significance. That idea couldn't be farther from the truth. Our every action has *tremendous* ramifications in creation, though most of us refuse to observe and accept this.

For example, let's say a neuron in your brain suddenly realized that it was part of a sequence of neurons that, when fired sequentially, cause damage to itself and the neurons around it. Or that, upon discovering its "true" nature, realized it had been firing improperly, and so changes its pattern. By doing so, it influences the neurons around it, and so the pattern is altered.

What that neuron didn't realize was that it was part of the pattern that caused the larger physical manifestation, the *human being*, to overeat, causing many health and psychological problems. Its single heroic change altered the course of the entire human's life. We could go farther; perhaps that human becomes a symbol to others of achievement; perhaps, with a new self-confidence, they go on to motivate many others.

Being an integrated part of creation demands that *every action or thought is of monumental importance*, because it affects everything at every scale and position through interaction and chain reaction. In the new science of *chaos*, this is called the *Butterfly Effect*, where action at a relatively small scale can mushroom into large scale effects.

Large or small scale, though, are relative concepts that disable us from seeing the vast importance of our actions on a day to day, moment by moment basis. Every action has immense ramifications, ringing like vibrations from a bell out through creation, causing reactions and chain reactions. Most of us, though, simply refuse to honestly observe this quality of reality, that we are interconnected with all of creation and our every action is of vital importance to the infinite dynamic of the universe. We, at our scale and position, are representational of the "whole" of reality, in that we are both a manifestation of infinite parts and are ourselves part of infinite systems. Our responsibility in life is to act true to our inner dynamic, in harmony with creation's dynamic forces, fulfilling our purpose at our scale and position. This harmonious interaction between ourselves and the universe releases us from the constricting belief systems and ideas that limit the *scale of our effective existence*, allowing us to *transcend* to a broader, higher manifestation.

H ere again we see that it is the socially-constructed *evaluation center* of *our* ego that limits us, or categorizes our existence according to a pathetically limited perception of reality. When we do come across evidence that our actions have broad, unforeseen ramifications, our ego interprets that information according to its pre-existing view of ourselves and life — by ignoring it, or calling in the phantom explanations of "luck" or "coincidence," instead of *re-organizing its self-view according to the observation itself*.

For example, I met my wife through an ad in a "personals" column. She wrote in the ad exactly what she wanted, physically and mentally, in a man. She had no trouble meeting and dating men, but figured she'd ask exactly for what she wanted. I enjoyed reading through the ads, and saw an ad with my exact description. We met, fell in love, and got married.

Here, we see that the consequences of seemingly trivial actions have tremendous impact. There are infinite examples of both tragedy and miracles occurring from seemingly inconsequential actions, either directly or from sequential, seemingly unrelated events. It happens all the time in all of our lives, and history is made up of monumental events that sprang from the most casual of causes.

This is easily understood when we accept the aforementioned structure of creation, or that of a *hierarchy* of interlocking, interdependent systems that stretch out infinitely through every direction and dimension. How can any action that any part of that hierarchy takes *not* have tremendous impact?

A single cell in our body becoming cancerous can have far reaching, dramatic impact, not only on the host's life, but on those around him or her. A single antibody, by simply *fulfilling its inherent, designed purpose,* can prevent the tragedy that cancer cell could cause. What if the antibody refused to kill the cell, deciding it was "morally" wrong? What if the antibody was busy building a cellular "home" for its "children" and didn't want to take the risk of losing its "security" by taking on the cancer cell? What if the antibody had been convinced by the cancer that its "true responsibility" was carrying iron through the blood stream like the red blood cells?

All these evaluations simply prevent the antibody from performing its assigned task, disrupting the perfect "flow" of creation. We each have our assigned tasks, our dynamic purpose, that is of equal importance to all other systems, at any scale and position. The whole concept of triviality is simply an excuse, a justification for fulfilling the program of society and satisfying the desires of the ego and ignoring the impulses of the *truth* within each of us.

Wherever a man goes, men will pursue him and paw him with their dirty institutions, and, if they can, constrain him to belong to their desperate oddfellow society.

— **Henry David Thoreau, 1817-1862**

Any institution which does not suppose the people good, and the magistrate corruptible, is evil.

— **Maximilien Robespierre, 1758-1794**

SOCIAL REALITY

The interconnectedness of all things, the relativity of *scale* and *position*, and the dynamic of our inherent, designed purpose are easily observable structures and principles that guide our life in the universe. Seeing reality any other way requires a colossal combination of *arrogance* and *ignorance*; to assume that we perceive any better a portion of reality than does an ant, or an amoeba, or than did primitive man; to ignore our integral physical, mental, and spiritual relationship to, and dependence upon, all the other systems in creation, both external and internal; and to subscribe to society's arbitrary agenda, assuming that it, though obviously destructive and ineffective, knows a better course of action for us than our own inner dynamic, which was instilled by and is a reflection of creation itself.

Any society's current mythology represents the parameters of the "real world" to its citizens. We refuse to see that this view is simply society's *current definition* of reality, which changes drastically over the years. "Reality" is not a concrete substance that can be defined, or else it would long ago have been established. *Reality is whatever it is perceived to be by an observer at a particular scale and position.*

"Society" is such an observer, and its perception of reality largely defines the world for its citizens. The more rigid a social mythology, the quicker the flowing, changing creation outdates it, rendering it incapable of effecting a harmonious relationship between creation and its citizens. The individual becomes out of sync with the dynamic, causing frustration, anger, and mental and physical disease to spread and intensify.

Every natural fact is a symbol of some spiritual fact.
— **Ralph Waldo Emerson, 1803-1882**

Rules and models destroy genius and art.
— **William Hazlitt, 1778-1830**

Like that of leaves is a generation of men.
— **Homer, 8th cent. B.C.**

SYMBOLS ARE REALITY

The "real world" cannot be defined outside of the principles that guide its existence, because every aspect of it is an infinite set of *symbolic manifestations* that exist *relative to the scale and position of the observer*. The principles that govern reality are actually the principles that *form and drive symbolic systems and the observer's interpretation of them*.

Any society that attempts to "define" the "real world" for its constituents is both ineffective and destructive, because any such definitions are only misleading and limiting.

A *symbol* is the representation, as a single entity, of a multitude of component parts. For example, the American flag is a symbolic representation of the fifty states; an atom is symbolic of the sub-atomic quantum field relationships of its component particle/waves; and the concept of "*honor*" is symbolic of a behavioral pattern that involves hundreds of everyday occurrences and possibilities. While a symbol is composed of many parts and exhibits the behavior of a single, total entity, the symbol exists *only to a particular observer (or observers) at certain positions and scales*. The same component parts can be observed as many different symbolic entities, depending on the scale and position of the observer. Further, the symbolic entity is always a component part of a higher symbolic entity; the American flag is but one flag of many nations on the Earth, the atom is a component part of many substances; and honor could be the component part of an individual, an organization's code of conduct, or perhaps an idea in a book.

The brain is a physical tool constructed of about ten billion neurons and a hundred billion glial cells. Data is manipulated in the brain through sequential and group neuron "firing," or electro-chemical stimulation. Though we do not have control over each individual neuron, nor even consciously know which groups or sequences of neurons are firing, we *can* control and manipulate our thoughts, mental imagery, and actions.

How is this possible? We are completely unconscious of the necessary mechanisms at the neuron and glial cell level, yet we go on about our day, thinking and taking action.

We are able to achieve action and thought through *symbol manipulation*. In other words, we command our bodies to stand and walk; those commands are *symbolic* of all the necessary cellular functions involved in the process of standing and walking. The broad symbolic command, or conscious thought, is broken up into lower level commands, below our conscious control, that actually activate the firing of the necessary groups and sequences of cells. Each action we command sets in motion a set of sub-commands that get the job done, with very little conscious activity whatsoever.

The *brain* can be said to be the actual "hardware," consisting of billions of cells. The *mind*, then, is composed of the symbols and symbol networks that we use to activate our neural processing. Since we cannot control each individual neuron (consider how many billions there are; the combinations would be infinite) any more than we could build a house molecule by molecule, we manipulate them via a vast storehouse of *symbols* which are easier to handle.

Using the house analogy, if the neuron level equates to the molecules of building materials, then the basic symbols of the mind equate to the tools and materials used in building a house. Lumber, bricks, mortar, nails, shingles, glass, tile, hinges; all these are basic, necessary materials when building a residence. We don't have to know how the molecules bind or interact or behave; that is inconsequential to us, because we know how to manipulate their larger manifestations — their *symbolic representations*.

The materials of our mind include the symbols that allow us to interpret and act. When hungry we seek food; when cold we seek warmth; when lonely we seek companionship. We don't understand any of the neural associations or pathways; understanding the component level is not necessary to think or act. Only understanding symbol manipulation is necessary.

Just as there are tools involved in manipulating the symbolic materials necessary to build a home, we all have tools within us to rearrange our mental materials. The greatest tool in our possession is observation, through which we can check to see if our symbolic representations of the world and our life in it are accurate, or are achieving what we want.

But tools are symbols as well. While we have observation, we also have tools that we ourselves have created to define those observations — *logic, reason, emotion, desire,* etc. These are tools of the ego that reside in our evaluation center and interpret creation according to our belief system. "We" are no longer in control of our own equipment; the machine that society programmed inside of us, the *ego,* is, and it uses our tools to protect and strengthen itself against our own desires.

The mind manipulates the various cells of our brain according to the symbols we call forth, or that are called forth by outside influences. Is it just the brain cells that these symbols manipulate?

O bviously not. Terror elicits adrenal stimulation; love causes endorphin production; anger releases acids and other harmful ingredients into the body. The medical community is in agreement that our mental state has a large amount of influence over our physical well-being. Stress and frustration have been documented to impair the immune system, allowing a host of ailments to attack us from within.

The brain is attached to and controls *every aspect of our physical body*; it constantly monitors and adjusts all our internal mechanisms. Each of us, though, perceive different situations as scary, stressful, or joyous. So, while we are all hard-wired basically the same, the *arrangement of our mental symbols* determines not only the firing pattern of neurons in the brain, but also the associative chemical production, release, and adjustment throughout our body. Therefore, by changing the way we interpret our observations through symbolic manipulation, we can completely alter the chemical patterns within our body.

Since the ego completely re-evaluates our observations to fit its agenda, the ensuing neural and chemical patterns are not in "tune" or harmony with ourselves or creation. The firing patterns and associative chemical adjustments mirror the interpretive qualities of our ego, our belief system. As shown before, that belief system is obviously false, inefficient, and destructive in its nature; the resulting physiological ramifications *must reflect those destructive, conflicting characteristics*.

In order to operate in the world, the mind must have within it a representation of itself — or of *us*. By simplifying the broad symbolic constructions into simple *personal characteristics* and collecting them together, our mental representation of ourselves, of who we are, what we look like, what we believe in, how we interact with the world, etc. is formed. This is the "I" that sits up on our mental throne and observes life.

The problem with this "I" is that it cannot seem to make its mental or physical body do what it wants it to do. It is a prisoner of *the way it is constructed, and what it is constructed from* — the ego. Bad habits cannot be changed, because they are built solidly into the stack of symbols that form the ego. Extracting the villain might undermine the entire "I" and create a weakness or even topple the entire construction. True change is virtually impossible, because it threatens our entire construction of symbols, or total self. Those that do attain real change rarely do so without having the entire structure broken down and reorganized into something new. The ego abhors the thought of breaking down and restructuring itself into a more effective, harmonious system, because that means accepting that its current construction is faulty, even destructive, and that many of its system arrangements are in error.

For us to accept change and to rearrange the symbolic patterns of our mind, we have to accept the pain and hurt of breaking down our systems of comforting beliefs, our views of self-worth and how we attain it, justifications of past actions and views, and so on. Breaking these symbol structures down is an extremely painful, frightening process, and the ego does not want to go through it.

Moreover, the mind protects itself by interpreting its observations in a way that supports its current construction. When evidence completely contradictory to the organization of the mind is observed and cannot be interpreted in a "friendly" way, it can be dumped or "unobserved" altogether. Our internal tools of logic, reason, etc., are used *not to alter our symbolic system to fit the observation, but to re-interpret the observation to fit our current symbolic, or belief, system.* As time goes on, more and more of creation must be redefined according to our belief system, meaning also that the chemical processes in our body are not responding to the world accurately — they are reacting to the *processed* observation, altered to protect the *ego,* or our belief system.

Since creation is an ever-changing, flowing *dynamic*, we must be an ever-changing, ever-flowing entity to stay in harmony with it. That means that the "I," or the ego, must be prepared to change, or undergo system reorganization — birth, change, death, and rebirth. We have been trained to fear death and change, instead of welcoming it, by an ineffective, destructive society. So our ego latches onto a certain set of symbolic interpretations, or a belief system, and begins interpreting the universe around it to conform to its mental arrangement, becoming further and further out of harmony at every level, causing all sorts of physical, mental, and spiritual disorder. As creation moves and flows, the secure mindset we struggle to maintain springs more and more leaks, all the time constricting us from true interaction and observation, true learning and enlightenment.

The reason it is so frightening, the reason it is so hard to change or rearrange our ideas for the better is that we *do not understand precisely what we are doing or what is happening to us when we attempt to change* — the ego has a set of ill-defined, misconceived symbols about the way the mind works, how it affects the body, and how it operates in the world. Our society gives it a completely false and self-destructive view of itself and its position in reality, and of how it operates. This false, destructive view of itself is at the root of the ego's limitations, the individual's self- and world-destroying actions, and of much of mankind's mental and physical disorders.

Earlier we defined a *symbol* as the *representation of a certain arrangement of component parts as observed by a certain entity at a certain scale and position.* An example is this very paragraph you are reading. If you were to read it letter by letter, the text would have no meaning. The letters, in and of themselves, have no real meaning and provide us with no representative symbols. The next step up are the individual words. While they do have individual meanings, they must exist within the context of a string of such symbols to provide a high level of symbolic meaning.

So, you have the basic, virtually meaningless component letters, the first layer of symbolic *words*, then the next step up, or the *sentence*. The entire *paragraph* is representative of a certain idea — that *symbols* are the *meaningful interpretation* of the basic, component parts of the symbol.

We perceive the entire *universe*, and every portion of it, as symbolic manifestations of component parts. This has to do with the qualities of *position* and *scale*, which govern our presence in, and view of, reality.

No matter our multi-dimensional (including time) *position* in the cosmos, or our *scale* (how large, small, long-lived, or multi-dimensional an area of operation), creation follows the same observable design and purpose — *birth, change, death, and rebirth*. On any level that we exist, or combination of position and scale, a certain slice of the cosmos is observable to us. What we observe at any level will be *symbolic*, or the representational *sum* of basic component parts that, at that level, will be individually meaningless to us.

Take a stream, for example. In looking at a flowing stream, you don't ever stop to think about all the meaningless, basic parts that had to operate in unison to activate that image in your brain — and the brain is where you actually see the stream, not "over there," because all sensations are interpreted within.

The stream is composed of countless, meaningless (at least to us, at *our* scale and position) atomic particles. The light reflecting off of the stream is composed of countless, meaningless photons. The photons interact with thousands of optical cells, which in turn activate large volumes of brain cells, which in turn represent the image to you, the observer. The image is symbolic of the billions of particles and interactions that were actually involved in the process.

Through this demonstration one can easily see that what we observe throughout life are symbolic representations of reality that are composed of an unimaginable number of elemental parts. The symbols themselves manifest to observing techniques (visual, audio, smell, machine, etc.) according to our position and scale. If we were much smaller or larger, the stream would appear quite different to us. If our optic cells were constructed differently, or if we had different processing equipment in our brain, we might not perceive the stream as a stream at all, but as something quite different.

I t is important to understand that everything we perceive is a symbolic representation of a part of reality. We do not perceive *all* of the object or concept, we observe only a very limited portion at a certain position and scale. Whether or not the "object" or "concept" exists *at all* in reality is meaningless. Even if it does, we perceive so inconsequential a portion of it in the infinite continuum of time, space, and the other dimensions that we can only regard it as a *representative symbol meant only for our observation*. Trying to find out what "it" *really* is, is like trying to find out what the "basic" sub-atomic particles are, or how the universe was created — it's a waste of time, because of the infinite nature of reality, and the fact that, no matter how far or deep we attempt to observe creation, because of the relativity of *position* and *scale*, we are observing no greater an amount of reality than we did before. All that is important is understanding the symbolic nature of what we observe, and that it reflects the nature of reality at every scale and position. Chasing ever smaller, or larger, or farther, or pre-historic scientific or religious "rainbows" is without true spiritual value, because all the information necessary to understand creation is available at every time and place, at every scale.

The nature of our existence is *symbolic*, in that everything we are, do, and perceive is symbolic in nature. Just as we cannot "see" or understand the *billions* of parts that make up every action, object, or thought, we have no idea what ultimate form our actions or thoughts will take, or the repercussions they will have. To other observers, our every action and word are component parts of their universe, and we have no idea how they perceive reality, how they interpret the *representational symbols* our actions and words are component parts of. We are parts of infinite symbolic structures we cannot see, because we can only view reality from our own perspective — what others see is beyond our ability to interpret. By acting according to our true, inner dynamic, though, we know that we are exhibiting exactly what creation, or the infinite Entity, *wants* other observers to perceive.

We have been trained by society to feel that symbols are of no substance; in reality, symbols are all that exist on any scale and at any position. Symbols *are* reality. Everything we think or do amounts to the manipulation of symbolic manifestations.

Man seeketh in society comfort, use, and protection.
— **Francis Bacon, 1561-1626**

Custom, then, is the great guide of human life.
— **David Hume, 1711-1776**

Big Brother is watching you.
— **George Orwell, *1984***

SOCIETY: A SYMBOLIC ENTITY

Society is an organic, symbolic system in this universe, like any other, made up of smaller systems and itself a part of much larger systems. As a system, like a human *cell*, it has its mechanistic parts that participate in keeping the system running. It generates its own self-perpetuating DNA for its "cells" in the form of mythic programming, or knowledge; this DNA is comprised of many encoded beliefs, such as *responsibility, security, ego, triviality,* and its definition of the *real world.*

It also has a *border,* much like a cell has its cell wall, that keeps the entire society together. This wall is constructed out of a variety of concepts and ideas and represents a kind of *fail-safe device* to keep members within the flock when all else fails. Included within this fail-safe "wall" are a whole host of concepts including *luck, religion, philosophy, statistics, chance, fate, destiny, paranormal, supernatural, averages, superstition, good, evil,* etc. What all these ideas have in common is that they are used to explain the *fallacies* inherent in our societies. They explain why things don't work out the way society has promised, and why we should not hold society accountable for it. They are *catch-all* explanations and justifications that we are told we should expect as part of reality. They are not truly part of "reality" at all, but only symbolic manifestations of the "wall," or of the limitations of society itself.

When we see things in life that are inexplicable, that our society has no answer for, it falls back to this perimeter line of defense and pulls out religion, or luck, or statistics to drop the wool over our eyes. These laughable, inane "reasons" are given when we ask why the world just doesn't act like society has programmed us to believe it would and why our actions don't bring the promised results.

As society falls further and further out of touch with reality, it attempts to further and further *define* or *restrict* reality to meet with its own agenda or construction. It finds itself caught in many self-conflicting, self-destructive patterns as it tries harder and harder to enforce its security and knowledge. Just as an individual causes himself harm by refusing to accept reality, so too society does itself harm — it is every bit as "real" as a physical symbolic manifestation, and behaves according to the same principles and structure of creation.

We have seen how all things are part of an infinite hierarchy of evolving, changing systems, or a universal *organism*. We have seen that this system is sustained through *time* as well as *space*, and how everything we observe of this universal, infinite *Entity* is a representational, symbolic *manifestation* of the Entity itself. *Everything* behaves according to and is constructed of the same principles and materials of creation.

We also know that much of the universe cannot be experienced through our pathetically limited five senses. We can extend the range of these senses through various types of *observational equipment* we create — telescopes, radarscopes, electron microscopes, infrared and radio-wave receptors, etc. However, the universe has taught us without fail the lesson that *regardless* of our observational capabilities, the universe looks pretty much the same from any vantage point in physical space as well as in *time*.

The point here is that our ability to observe the world through our five senses is shockingly limited. But, drawing from what we observe to be the true state of reality, *all things are part of the evolving hierarchy of systems.* This means that phenomena that exist outside of our sensory capabilities *must also* behave like the systems we *can* perceive.

This explains the hierarchy of the individual belief system within the societal belief system, and their relationship to each other. They are actual "organic" systems that behave exactly as physical organisms; they are born, they change, die, and are reborn in a different form. It is just that they exist as entities that are *not currently observable* except as effects in the physical realm, or the limited spectrum of phenomena that we are *able* to measure.

If we take the logical step that the individual is part of the greater system *mankind,* and mankind is part of the greater system *Earth,* then the next logical step is that our belief system *is* exactly what it so richly demonstrates that it is — another facet of the hierarchy of systems, existing in a universal strata that we have not yet uncovered with physical instrumentation.

The hierarchy of systems exists in time and space, and in many ways we cannot observe with physical tools. Physical tools can only examine that which exists in or directly affects the physical aspects of the universe. If one is going to assume that anything other than an incredibly *insignificant* portion of creation is physically observable, one might as well believe that the Earth is the center of the cosmos and the universe revolves around it. In order to obey the *hierarchy* rule present throughout reality, *mental* phenomena *must* behave similarly — to believe otherwise is just to arbitrarily step outside of the observable conditions of reality.

So, we can understand that a society is an organic system that is comprised of smaller systems and itself is part of a larger system. How does this aid in our understanding of the destructiveness of its current behavior?

By looking at similar models and understanding how they behave. Take, for example, many of the bacterial and viral organisms that exist in man. *E. coli*, for example, is an organism that probably began as an extremely destructive entity, killing thousands, if not millions, before it mutated into an organism that is actually *beneficial* to the digestive processes of man, and became part of our genetic code.

Think of the flu viruses and other epidemic-type of entities that strike man in great numbers. No sooner do we grow resistant to one strain of flu than a hardier strain emerges. No sooner do we defeat one type of disease than another type emerges. That these diseases have an *evolutionary* effect on mankind is without question.

The flu, for instance, is like a sparring partner for our immune system. Which comes away stronger and more robust after its encounter. The fight against *polio, rubella,* and *tuberculosis* led to the discovery of current inoculation techniques, which in effect give our immune system weakened opponents to fight in order to be ready if the stronger version rears its head.

These diseases and organisms were evolutionary processes, either directly mutating into beneficial beings (out of the desire not to destroy their host) or causing mankind to develop new ideas and understanding.

Mental organisms behave in the same way, and looking at them as such uncovers much of the mystery surrounding mental phenomena. *Ideas* are freshly born mental organisms that evolve, die, and are reborn in a different form. If this nascent organism is vital and serves a need of the larger organism, it will thrive, even if its presence changes the nature of the larger mental system of the individual and of the larger system of *society*.

It is easy to see that in the same way that physical epidemics have swept through vast portions of mankind, so have *ideas*. In the same way that physical organisms can be transferred from one host to another *physically*, ideas and more complex mental organisms can be transferred *mentally*, through simple observation and communication.

Freedom, democracy, Islam, Christianity, socialism, communism, aggression, equality, and environmentalism are all examples of complex idea organisms that demonstrate the process of birth, change, death, and rebirth. These belief systems compete against each other and vie for supremacy, eventually giving way, in time, to better suited and hardier belief systems.

What makes one mental organism hardier than another? Its ability to survive and reproduce, spreading to other hosts. If it is able to not only live in harmony with its host but actually *becomes an essential part of its continued existence*, then it has succeeded as well as *E. coli*, without which we could not live as long nor digest the variety of foodstuffs we do now. Though *E. coli* was at first destructive, it evolved into an ally. An *essential* ally.

Now the processes of society are easily understood. Through history, we have seen social birth, change, death, and rebirth, not just of ideas but of entire social *systems*, as these systems meet competition from outside and are mutated by ideas from within. The desired end product is a system that is in harmony with its host on every scale — individual, social, planetary, etc.

Society is destructive, then, in the same way that *E. coli* was destructive: it is part of an evolutionary process that transforms both its component parts and the larger system into a more harmonious set of systems. Like any other viral infection that destroys or incapacitates its host body or bodies, given time, it will evolve into a harmonious entity.

Given time, so would, in all likelihood, smallpox, rubella, polio, etc. Instead, we addressed those organisms directly with evolutionary steps of our own and devised a different way of looking at disease and our resistance to it with *immunology* and *inoculation*. To prevent social disorder from running rampant, destroying individuals, countries, and perhaps disabling the planet from being able to support us, we must take a great evolutionary step forward and change the way we look at reality and ourselves. The inadequacies and destructive nature of society are forcing us to evolve, just as disease forced us to evolve, into a new way of looking at the world and ourselves.

J ust as any organism resists change, society is slow and sluggish when adopting new ideas and beliefs. Society *does* change, each evolutionary step slow, methodical, *painful*. However, there is strong evidence that society, like any organism, cannot change its fundamental *principles* without the process of *death* and *rebirth*.

When you think of the fall of the Roman Empire, the fall of the British Empire, and the fall of the Soviet Union, you see the sweeping consequences of systems that are unable to change their fundamental *myths* when hardier ideas are developed. Society by and large seeks out these new myths and attempts to destroy them, like any organism that perceives a threat, from within or from an outside agent. It is the process of competition and natural selection which is so evident in the world.

What, really, is so wrong with our society that it indicates something as drastic as death and rebirth? It might be argued that the free-enterprise/democratic system is an organism *designed* for change when a better idea comes along.

That our system was originally a vast improvement over the various forms of dictatorships and elitism cannot be argued. It represented a *tremendous* leap forward for the individual, giving him or her unparalleled power to choose their own life as they saw fit, to live true to their designed purpose. But, like other societies in the past, certain commonly held beliefs have, over time and circumstance, come to be regarded as *unassailable truth*. While these fallacies were not tremendously destructive at one time (if you didn't like it, you could find a relatively uninhabited place to hang your hat), the situation of the modern world is vastly different.

Leaving is no longer a true option. We really can't sail across the ocean or head west anymore if we run into persecution or ridicule. Modern, crowded Earth has become like a pressure cooker, boiling up the base elements that make us ineffective and destructive creatures, no longer affording us the opportunity to leave the old, decrepit belief system behind.

That our society is *fundamentally* inefficient is horribly obvious. We are a nation of wealth, yet within our borders, many of us go hungry, homeless, or without basic medical care. We gleefully *persecute* those with beliefs or habits unlike our own, whether they be blacks, feminists, gays, Jews, New Agers, trans-sexuals, etc. We destroy the environment, giving pause only when our own *survival* is at stake.

An unbelievably large percentage of our population is addicted to drugs, both legal and not. Another huge segment is behind bars, becoming even more anti-social awaiting their release. Society does not even attempt to rehabilitate its wayward citizens; how many of those behind bars are there strictly due to economic needs or physical addictions?

We are a society that is told, by and large, that our only goal is individual happiness and satisfaction, and that the only way to attain this goal is by accumulating *more*. In our mad desire to have *more*, we pay little attention to that which we discard, who suffers because of our self-centered quest, or even why we never reach our goal, no matter how *much* we accumulate.

We are a nation of mentally unbalanced individuals, of drug addicts, alcoholics, black-lunged smokers, anorexics and life-long dieters, schizophrenics, paranoiacs, manic-depressives, co-dependent enablers, hurt inner-children, spouse abusers, child abusers, co-worker harassers, employee harassers, workaholics, criminals, ozone destroyers, killers of innocent animals, gang members, cultists, bigots, self-righteous fundamentalists, sociopaths, women who hate men, men who hate women, religious fanatics, science worshippers, idol worshippers, violent, passive-aggressive people... and we have the *gall* to lock up certain *other* individuals for going "over the line."

It is a society that is buckling under its own weight. Unable to leave, we are forced to see that our views are not *divine* or *inspired*, just another pathetic set of inefficient, self-contradictory beliefs that were programmed into us. Because of population and communication, we can no longer ignore the views of others or cling to the now obviously *ridiculous* notion that our beliefs are somehow inherently superior to everyone else's on this planet. Though we consciously block out the massive amount of information that demands our entire belief system be junked, our subconscious can no longer stand up under the strain. There is just too much conflicting information that it cannot ignore or move away from or dump into its "aberrant" file.

Our society is an organism quickly approaching the stage of *death* and *rebirth*, as evidenced by its inability to serve the needs of its individual constituents. It has grown cumbersome, static, inefficient, and destructive, and so *must* be removed and replaced.

When any physical organism displays the above traits, it is surely headed for death and replacement, either from within or at the hands of hardier organisms outside.

Our society is founded on the notion of stability and security, of responsibility and ego, of triviality and the "real world." We are all completely indoctrinated into this way of life; imagine trying to reform our society so that it reflects the true nature of reality, which is exactly the *opposite* of those concepts.

The collapse of our society is not just inevitable, it is a *necessity*, so that a new foundation can be erected, one that reflects *reality* and allows individuals to express their inner dynamic freely, instead of *enslaving* them physically, mentally, and emotionally. This collapse is not something that must be aided in any way; it is better for all organisms if death arrives *naturally* as it meets competitors from within and outside. However, by subscribing to the structure of society and attempting to sustain it we contribute to its ability to become even more outdated and destructive. The longer it goes on, the more complete and devastating its collapse will be.

From a historical and common-sense viewpoint, a collapsing society going through death and rebirth can best be described as a violent and tumultuous time. As the economic and ideological pillars that support a culture collapse and reform, there is always panic and strife. The masses that have been completely indoctrinated by the program of the old, crashing society can rarely change, becoming angry, violent, or even going mad. Only those open to change fare the transition with equanimity, keen interest, even a sense of opportunity.

The problem of building a new social order is apparent when there is naught but the ruins of the old or of barely better outside cultures to model the new one by. *A new order of thinking is necessary*, much like the new order that created democracy and the free-enterprise system, an order that *embraces* the true form of reality: the infinite hierarchy of systems, observable only as symbolic manifestations at any scale or position, completely inter-connected and inter-dependent, driven by a universal *dynamic* of system reorganization, and the divine nature of the *transcendent individual* within that hierarchy.

It is the customary fate of new truths to begin as heresies and to end as superstitions.

— T. H. Huxley, 1825-1895

Everything flows and nothing stays.

— Heraclitus, 5th cent. B.C.

The longest journey is the journey inwards of him who has chosen his destiny, who has started his quest.

— Dag Hammarskjold, 1905-1961

UNDERSTANDING OURSELVES

Understanding the nature of reality, we also understand the nature of our own *identity*. Who we view ourselves as and what we do in the world is defined by the complex symbolic patterns within our mind. How, then, may we transcend our own identity, and grow into something larger, something unlimited, unafraid of any threat or intimidation? Something that can withstand the tumultuous times of a failing society?

An atom is composed of symbolic patterns. So are molecules, cells, and organs, such as the brain. At the sub-atomic level, we find no "hardware" — all particles exist as "wave probabilities." Only when we enter our realm of positions and scales do things become "real" and take on physical form, like the brain. Mental activity can be explained as an electro-chemical process, just as sub-atomic activity can be explained as quantum interactions. I like to refer to the sub-atomic world as the *infra-physical world*, and mental or spiritual activity as the *ultra-physical* world. They are phenomena that exist below and above our ability to monitor by physical means, because they exist *outside of our realm of position and scale*, the physical world. The most we can monitor is their respective *effects* on our realm.

W e, as individuals, exist in a symbolic format riding electro-chemical processes in our physical brain, just as our entire physical world exists in symbolic format riding on the quantum processes underneath it. The physical world is no less real because of it, and so neither are we. I'm sure there is a sub-quantum level that supports the quantum, which supports the physical arena, and so forth.

Our mental processes, then, *must support a higher level of reality* that is every bit as "real" as any other level when viewed from that perspective, of which we, as individuals, are *component parts*. Remember, component parts are not limited to *one* symbolic manifestation, but are involved in a multitude of higher symbols, depending on how and from where they are being observed.

One such "higher level" that we as individuals are component parts of is *our society*, which in turn is a component part of *humanity*. Every action by every individual throughout time can be said to be the component parts of humanity, or the present state of mankind. Humanity is a component part of the world community of organisms, of which the Earth is the symbolic manifestation.

Does this greater hierarchy of symbol manifestations indicate that we, as individual, component parts, are meaningless? Well, when viewed from a planetary scale, the actions of any single human appear quite meaningless, like the individual letters on a page of text. We shouldn't despair that our lives are therefore pointless, though.

Let us follow the metaphor of an individual resembling a letter on a page of a book. The letter represents an individual action at a certain time; perhaps, over the course of a lifetime, the individual's presence on Earth takes on the expanded meaning of an entire word of text in the chapter of "society" in the book of "humanity."

A single word can change the meaning of all the words that surround it; they in turn change the meaning of the entire text. We have the power in life to have a profound effect on the universe, if our word is strong, bold, and precise. Our life takes on a powerful *symbolic meaning* that has far-reaching consequences.

In order to fulfill the full symbolic meaning of our individual identities, we must be able to grow and change as the world around us does so, maintaining our symbolic meaning in an ever-changing environment. Otherwise, our meaning will be lost because the *context*, or environment, will have changed, and we will be left with unusable ideas and beliefs. This is the security that lies within ourselves; though the world changes, we implement our inner symbolic nature accordingly.

This is a partial explanation of *transcendence*; by accepting the dynamic nature of the text around us, we do not limit ourselves to a certain sentence — i.e., a certain scale and position. The ability to fluidly change grants us a wider, higher symbolic meaning in the text of society and humanity. Instead of being a *neuron*, limited to a certain physical position and a certain set of actions, we become a *symbol*, a tool that can be effective in a wider variety of situations and has greater access, or a larger realm of scale and position.

So transcendence is the raising of oneself from the meaningless, restricted level of a component part to that of a symbolic representation. Logically, transcendence from one level to the next of symbolic manifestation can be carried on infinitely, or as long as there are higher symbolic manifestations to "transcend" towards.

The transcendence of one's consciousness, however, is not limited to the transformation from the individual perspective to that of the societal, human, or global view.

A single neuron in the brain, if it could view itself consciously (and there is no proof that it doesn't), could choose to see itself in many different ways — as an individual with its own agenda that it pursues of its own accord; a representative of a group of symbols that it has immense personal power to affect; a member of a biological eco-sphere called the human body that it has a responsibility to help maintain, and so on. If the neuron limits itself to a low, strictly physical understanding of itself, then it is limited to acting in the way the higher symbolic patterns dictate — all the time, of course, believing it is acting according to its own desires. By "transcending" its perception of itself, the neuron becomes more than a neuron — it understands itself as a part of a network of neurons that are in turn part of many symbolic patterns that govern the mental and physical makeup of its reality — the human body.

We are taught by society to view ourselves as individual entities within a certain context of systems we are responsible to help maintain, whether or not those systems affect us in a constructive or *destructive* way. The fact is that we are no more isolated individuals than each of the billions of cells that make up our bodies are isolated individuals, or are the countless molecules that each cell is constructed of.

There is no such thing as an isolated individual; everything is composed of systems and in turn is part of many higher systems. At any level of the system, a certain organization of symbolic representations gives rise to consciousness, or the representation of the self within the symbolic patterns (more accurately, the representation of a *portion* of the self).

Even within a single brain there can be many "egos," as in the case of those with multiple personalities. Many of us have different parts of our mind — our *conscience*, for example — that vie for supremacy when deciding upon an action. Many of us *are* split into several different identities — one that represents our concept of *ideal behavior*, one that tempts us into *desired behavior*, and a third part that negotiates between the two.

Those of us that find our minds tugged in many different directions are at the mercy of conflicting mental symbol structures that constantly fight for control of our thoughts and actions. The split between ideal and desired behavior is the result of the dualistic nature forced upon the individual by society; we divide things into good and evil, right and wrong, pro and con, and so forth. While one symbol network of neurons in our brain struggles to keep us from taking a "forbidden" action, another network, perhaps the *pleasure network*, prompts us to take the action.

In fact, since all systems follow the same principles, we can, with complete assurance, say the mind is an entity composed of countless sub-systems and an infinite number of "component parts," just like our physical body. To view our mind as something different than what is so universally displayed in creation is a crippling disability.

Just like our physical body is a collection of inter-dependent organic entities on many different levels, so our mind is a vast hierarchy of thought systems, each sub-system being "alive" and, on its own level, an individual entity. This concept is critical to understanding ourselves and paving the way toward our transcendence and enlightenment, releasing the bonds that tie us to the decaying society around us.

Any individual entity in creation is comprised of an infinite hierarchy of subsystems and is part of an infinite number of "larger" systems. This means that *we are not one being, but a collection of entities that manifest, at our scale and position, as a single entity or individual.*

If we were red blood cells, then all cells in our universe (the human body) would look like whole individuals to whatever perceptive technique we had at that level. Even though we, as a cell, and all our cell friends were comprised of an infinite number of cellular sub-structures (nucleus, DNA, RNA, ribosomes, lysosomes, mitochondrion, golgi apparatus, endoplasmic reticulum, chloroplasts, the cell wall, etc.), we would see each other as separate, distinct beings, doing whatever we wish within the condition of our environment.

Our minds are constructed of many different entities with different agendas and programmings. Though our physical organs are all programmed differently, that different-ness is what keeps the entire body functioning smoothly, harmoniously — *unless a harmful, destructively-programmed element* begins generating disharmony and destruction, spreading its harmful influences throughout our body and conflicting with the smooth running of the various systems.

Even though each sub-system is designed to follow different processes, if they are allowed to do so, to exhibit their *individually designed inherent dynamic* without restriction, without suppression, without re-programming, then, as a whole, the widely varying systems function in complete perfection and harmony.

The different "organs" and "cells" (concepts and thoughts) of our minds are unable to manifest this perfect dynamic because of the destructive influence of society. The myths and belief systems we are subjected to from birth are toxic entities that vilify and ridicule our *inherent dynamic*, demanding that we restructure our mental nature according to *its* blueprint. The problem is that only our natural dynamic is a reflection of *all the infinite forces at work in creation*, and so is in harmony with every impulse and action at every scale and position. The artificial blueprint of society takes into account only what it can observe when making its demands and decisions. Since what it can observe is only an insignificant portion of creation, and it doesn't base its guidelines on the underlying principles that guide reality, its agenda will unerringly prove destructive.

Because all of our natural impulses have been re-written and many completely false programs have been inserted into our mental body, we find ourselves in complete mental disarray. We argue with ourselves unceasingly. We are easily confused and manipulated. We have no control over our own actions and habits. This destructive chaos and confusion manifests in our bodies as a whole host of problems and ailments because of the conflicting and self-destructive chemical processes they activate throughout our various physical systems.

We find ourselves, many times, as the mere observer in our minds, forced to watch while more powerful entities in us force us into action we know is harmful or inefficient. We argue, and blame, and cry, and justify, and bitch, and scream, because we have no tools, no help, no way to deal with it, no understanding whatsoever of what is going on.

By developing a conceptual, symbolic understanding of ourselves and creation around us, we nurture a powerful ally, an entity of infinite power within our minds to help us transform ourselves and our lives, to give us the ability to *transcend* our current self-destructive, socially imposed limitations.

Our life always expresses the result of our dominant thoughts.

— **Soren Kierkegaard, 1813-1855**

There is nothing good or bad, but thinking makes it so.

— **William Shakespeare, *Hamlet***

Two men look out through the same bars: one sees the mud, and one the stars.

— **Frederick Langbridge, 1849-1923**

TRANSCENDING SOCIALLY IMPOSED LIMITATIONS

The mental programming that society has indoctrinated us with, being in direct conflict with our inner, perfect *dynamic*, and the guiding principles of reality, creates disharmony and self-conflict within the organization of our "individual" mental community.

Ego, that entity within us that endlessly categorizes and evaluates phenomena according to the social blueprint, could also be called our *evaluation center*. It is critical to understand that, like every other symbolic manifestation in creation, *Ego* is an actual entity comprised of infinite subsystems and part of our community mind, as well as an obedient member of whatever portion of society we belong to. We have been trained by society to give Ego control of virtually every function, mental or physical, because through it society holds total control over us.

By *transcending* the level of the *evaluation center*, we have raised our identities to a point that symbolically understands Ego and its place in our "individual" community mind. To transcend, we let go of the rigid notions and opinions through which the Ego keeps us locked into place, and move to a higher symbolic array.

By understanding that the Ego/evaluation center is society's programmed agent within us, we start to realize why we are so fractured and confused. The information supplied to the Ego by its greater system, society, is terribly incomplete and limited, in direct conflict with the natural perfection of creation. Because society/Ego cannot explain why its program doesn't work, it must start finding "reasons" that support its own self worth through justification and blame. It splits everything into good and bad, positive and negative, right and wrong, true and false, justifying its inadequacies and finding fault in that which does not support it.

By detaching ourselves from the Ego, simply by realizing what it is, we can see its evaluations for what they are. This has always been a hard process in the past, because people saw the Ego as *themselves* — another great trick of society. Ego is like a masterful parasite that has hypnotized us into thinking that *it is who we are*, hiding from us our own nature as a hierarchical collection of entities, of which Ego is but *one*, though it has infested much of the rest of our mental community with its destructive reprogramming.

By understanding the principles outlined in the first part of this book, we can transcend the area where the Ego dominates us and see that all of its knowledge and evaluations serve only to fracture and confuse us, maintaining society's control over our lives. We move to a level where we view creation not according to the conflicting, destructive, limited perspective of the Ego, but as a harmonious, perfect reality that Ego, and its parent, society, prevent us from realizing and interacting with honestly.

Only those means of security are good, are certain, are lasting, that depend on yourself and your own vigor.

 — Machiavelli, 1469-1527

True and False are attributes of speech, not of things. And where speech is not, there is neither Truth nor Falsehood.

 — Thomas Hobbes, 1588-1679

The secret of success is consistency of purpose.

 — Benjamin Disraeli, 1804-1881

CREATION IS PERFECT

Just as symbolic sub-atomic manifestations can be interpreted as opposites (particles or waves), so can phenomena that exist at other scales and positions. Good and evil, in our evaluation center, are simply definitions that limit our perception of ourselves and the universe. Just as all sub-atomic phenomena are *both* **waves** *and* **particles**, depending only upon how they are *observed*, so too are all actions and thoughts good *and* evil, right *and* wrong, valuable *and* worthless, etc. Our evaluation center can be transcended by understanding how it splits harmonious concepts into opposites and chooses, thereby *justifying our actions and motives by "picking" the "right" action,* and condemning the "wrong" action. Right action is justified and falsely increases self-worth; wrong action is blamed and, again, falsely increases or decreases our self-image.

For years scientists tried to prove that there were either "particles" or "waves" that supported our physical world; the two camps fought each other bitterly, each claiming they were "right" and the other "wrong." Eventually, they all had to admit that the *evidence gathered depended upon the position and scale of the observation itself, not the phenomena, which displayed whatever characteristics the tests were meant to find.*

This is the same problem that society faces as it attempts to mentally and physically enforce its existence; by existing in the arena of evaluated choices — right and wrong, knowledge and superstition, etc. — it uses these evaluations to explain its restrictions and decisions and then must, at some point, take an action that conflicts with a previous explanation. Then, of course, the justifications and more complicated explanations must follow, which will, of course, conflict with a current or future situation.

Removing such restrictions moves us to a higher level, from which we don't view actions or events as good and right or bad and wrong. On this level, we have transcended our old set of fractured and conflicting ideas that caused us so much pain and confusion. Though action is still taken, we do not evaluate or judge it according to our old, stringent, simplistic values, but merely accept action and the ramifications thereof as part of the whole, no longer having the need to label the action or results with moralistic or ethical meaning.

Transcendence, then, is moving from one scale where opposites appear, to a higher one where those opposites are co-existent and harmonious. It is the shedding of conflicting evaluations that hide the perfection of creation from us. There are many avenues of transcendence. The raising of the physical viewpoint from that of the "isolated individual" in conflict with the world to the harmonious, integrated view of the self and creation around it; the escalation from a justification and blame, right vs. wrong decision making process to one that simply follows the urges of the inner dynamic, without interpretation or evaluation — these are two examples of possibly limitless ways in which we may seek personal transcendence.

If one advances confidently in the direction of his dreams, and endeavors to live the life which he has imagined, he will meet with a success unimagined in common hours.

— **Henry David Thoreau, 1817-1862**

Freedom is the right to choose; the right to create for yourself the alternatives of choice. Without the exercise of choice, a man is not a man but a member, an instrument, a thing.

— **Archibald MacLeish, 1892-**

HEROISM

Personal heroism can be defined as being *fearlessly true* to your inner self by finding and implementing your *designed purpose*. As explained earlier, everything in creation exhibits an inner, designed purpose that serves some necessary function. The fulfillment of these intrinsic, individual programs results in the order and harmony demonstrated by creation.

Mankind, on the other hand, appears at odds with himself and the world. *Society* overrides his natural purpose with its own program that defies and even vilifies the true structure of reality and his own desires, resulting in the disharmony and destruction so vividly apparent.

Rediscovering your designed purpose by stripping away the false programming of society, abandoning the aberrant belief systems, and embarking upon a path of honest observation and self-discovery is what is meant by the term *social disobedience*. *Heroism* is the process of *implementing* that inner purpose regardless of the so-called *ramifications* or perceived obstacles. Heroism can be achieved by moving beyond the *mental arena of evaluations*, the part of us that judges everything and classifies all events and thoughts according to our society-produced, dualistic, self-conflicting and fractured system.

Our inner purpose cannot be implemented accurately without moving beyond and getting rid of this system. That dynamic design within us is like a white light that shines through us; the evaluation center acts like a prism that breaks the dynamic into *perceived*, fractured *colors* that different societies label with various moral or ethical tags. The result is that the inner dynamic is repressed and misinterpreted because of our evaluation process. Since this design is *who we really are*, our inability to understand and fully implement it leaves us frustrated, angry, sick, depressed, etc. — because that dynamic is pure and demands to be heard and acted upon, but our *Ego* will not allow it to be free. This conflict is behind our every problem as individuals and as a species.

A *hero* is a person who moves beyond his physical limitations to represent an ideal; he or she becomes *symbolic* of a certain dynamic. Just as Lincoln represents fairness and freedom, Mother Theresa represents selflessness and love, and Hitler represents totalitarian intolerance, the ability lies within each of us to move beyond our self-imposed limitations into a higher, symbolic life, by living true to our inner design, regardless of the so-called *ramifications* or perceived obstacles. Heroism can be achieved by moving beyond the *mental arena of evaluations*, the part of us that judges everything and classifies all events and thoughts according to our society-produced, dualistic, self-conflicting and fractured system.

Though one would hardly call *Hitler* a hero, he was undeniably a symbolic manifestation of intolerance and nationalistic oppression. Remember, to many Germans at the time Hitler *was* a great hero. The way we view any symbolic person depends upon our point of view. Napoleon, Custer, Darwin, Jesus, Buddha, MacArthur, Stalin, Martin Luther King — all heroes and anti-heroes, depending upon your personal evaluation process. But their transcendence into a higher, symbolic nature cannot be refuted.

Just as the volcano and tornado exhibit their fundamental nature without regret or remorse, so do some humans. *Death, destruction,* and *sorrow* are as much a part of creation as *life, creation,* and *joy.* The "destructive" forces of nature are every bit as necessary as the constructive. To build the new, the old must fall. Life depends upon death. It is the eternal cycle of birth, change, death, and rebirth. It just depends on your position in the cycle as to whether or not you see the action as *birth* or *death.*

This is much of the reason behind our inability to find and implement our true purpose; our evaluation program defines our actions as positive or negative, good or evil, etc., prohibiting us from taking action that may *seem* wrong or "bad," even though we feel the need deep inside to take that action, or harbor that thought. We have vast *guilt* programming that prevents any exploration outside of the personal or social limitations on our behavior. Society doesn't recognize the cyclic nature of reality or the transient properties of *scale* and *position* in its machinations or agenda, leaving the individual without any true understanding of creation and his or her place in it, and our freedom to act — or *create* — as we please, as our inner design desires.

Heroism is necessary to find and implement your inner self, because that path means overcoming deep personal and social obstacles. It means literally *dying,* so that you may recreate yourself. This is the path of the mythological hero who faces and accepts death as a part of life and refuses to be cowed by it. It means going out on the *quest* — the true adventure of life, that of finding your divine self; seeking out the dragon — the terrible forces in your own mind that prevent you from attaining your divine status; and continually accepting *death* and *rebirth* — allowing your old concepts and beliefs to "die," so that your consciousness may be reborn into a larger, more effective nature.

Heroism is understanding that implementing your true, symbolic nature is what your purpose here in creation is all about. By implementing your heroic nature you achieve personal *transcendence*, allowing your mind to be continually broken down and recreated into higher symbolic patterns and activity. The *quest* can be embarked upon on a day to day, moment by moment basis, regardless of the position or scale one finds oneself in, because scale and position are *meaningless evaluations*. The true measure of the hero is simply the *degree to which he is implementing his personal dynamic*, at whatever scale and position he operates in.

Whatever you can do, or think you can, begin it. Boldness has genius, power, and magic in it.

— **Goethe, 1749-1832**

It is not easy to find happiness in ourselves, and it is not possible to find it elsewhere.

— **Agnes Repplier, 1858-1950**

Believe me! The secret of reaping the greatest fruitfulness and the greatest enjoyment from life is to **live dangerously!**

— **Nietzsche, 1844-1900**

OUR INNER DYNAMIC

Everything is a symbolic manifestation; every conscious entity interprets the manifestation according to their particular evaluation center. Every thought and action manipulates symbols around us, whether they are physical representations of subatomic, quantum fields or the mental patterns of individual neurons. Everything we *are* is like a multi-dimensional bell in creation, ringing and sending vibrations through symbolic worlds.

How our action will affect creation cannot be our concern, since that is unobservable to us. We don't know what the eventual ramifications will be, how other persons are being affected, consciously or subconsciously. We don't know what other events or thoughts will be added, mixed, or re-interpreted to our own to produce who-knows-what results. When we act, we don't know even a fraction of the forces that have led to the current situation, or how our words or action are going to interact with it.

Our only concern is to behave *according to our inner dynamic*, the force within us that guides and directs our life. This is the same as *having faith*, or *giving your life to God*, or any of a hundred other terms that describe the concept of personal *heroism*. It is dismissing the laughable idea that we can *evaluate* and *manipulate "reality"* in our day to day life, or understand its various manifestations and what they "really" mean, and instead simply *allowing our inner dynamic to flow outward into creation without restriction, alteration, or evaluation.* Through this dynamic inter-action with the universe we become a harmonious part of the whole, giving our life over to the designed purpose of the world.

Perhaps, before unchaining ourselves from our self-imposed restrictions and allowing this inner design to reign over our existence, we need a clearer under-standing of this inner dynamic and where it comes from. Most societies vilify this instinctual impulse and attempt to enforce an artificial, supposedly beneficial set of rules, both written and implied. It is therefore interesting to note that very few societies have lasted any great length of time, usually running a course of only a few score or perhaps hundreds of years. Societies may be formed to provide a better human condition; however, as a certain class of a society becomes comfortable and prospers, they attempt to keep the status quo, or manipulate the structure of the society to maintain or better their own position — neces-sarily at the increasing expense of other elements in the society.

In this way a society can be likened to a single human (remember, all symbolic systems at any scale reflect each other) as he or she grows comfortable within a certain position in the universe. When the time comes to change, or leave that security behind, they find they cannot — certain symbolic patterns within their own mind will not allow them to change, because they are not willing to give up their dominant position or pleasurable patterns — just like the aristocratic and powerful elements of our society will not relinquish the very patterns that are destroying our nation and the planet.

So, society cannot claim to be superior to the instinctual design of the individual. A society that is truly able to change and flow as the dynamic universe moves would be ideal — and that would certainly be in the best interest of all concerned, at any scale. As societies come and go, it is easy to observe a symbolic pattern that has been developing, moving from harsh, rigid, totalitarian forms of government and citizenry, toward a free, individualistic, open way of life. We have seen that the citizenry will not stand for oppressive government for very long, eventually bringing about its downfall. The innate forces and desires of the dynamic of creation, which exist in all of us, cannot be extinguished, or even dammed, for very long.

Like an individual who cannot forever ignore the forces of reality, even though they cling desperately to the "security" of a set of beliefs, comforts, and ideas, no society can remain "secure" within a certain set of rules, morals, ethics, and concepts forever. Creation *changes*, and so any symbolic representation must also change with it, or it gets further and further out of sync, becoming more and more dysfunctional and self-destructive.

From where does this inextinguishable, unstoppable, driving power come? It cannot be a result of the higher symbolic forces we are a part of, or our inner desires would mimic society's, and we would be happy and well adjusted performing its program. It must come from beyond the social manifestation level, because social orders are constantly being developed, rearranged, and destroyed as a result of its driving force.

This dynamic takes on an infinite variety of forms. It follows the implicit rule of creation, *system reorganization.* It recognizes no set belief pattern or program, and operates according to no ethical or moral guidelines, outside of any evaluation system.

The *shape* of creation is that of *symbolic manifestation.* Its *order*, or *function*, is *system reorganization*, or *birth, change, death*, and *rebirth.* The *power* that *reorganizes* creation's *symbolic manifestations* is that of the *universal dynamic.* It is the *essence* of life; it is behind every action that occurs, even though misinterpreted or largely repressed. It is the motivational energy that empowers all symbolic motion and change. *Nothing* occurs without this dynamic power's presence. Like the *shape* and *function* of creation, the *dynamic* is sewn into the fabric of reality. Those three actually *comprise* reality, reflecting *what reality is, how it works,* and *what empowers it.* The dynamic is the *Holy Ghost,* the *Will of God,* the *Music of the Spheres,* the *Word,* and can be called a hundred other names.

Trying to understand *what* it is is similar to trying to understand what exactly a symbolic manifestation *really* is, or what physical matter is *really* made up of, etc. The dynamic doesn't exist outside of its personal interpretation. What is important is accepting it as the guiding element of reality, because it cannot be defined outside of your personal interpretation of it. It has no defining qualities, no way of being assessed in any evaluation system. Like system reorganization and symbolic manifestation, trying to say what "it" really is means trying to define it according to a certain limited, "objective" evaluation process, which cannot define something both unlimited and ever-changing.

The dynamic can only be observed and accepted. It cannot be justified, proved, or defined. By observing the form, function, and dynamic of creation at work in every aspect of our existence, we gain the ability to reject evaluation processes, whether religious, philosophical, or scientific, and live *heroically,* without petty justification or guilt. We become truly *free,* unbour d by subjective programs and codes. We release our inner dynamic into creation, unafraid and uninhibited, allowing ourselves a harmonious unity with the universe.

More than that, we uncover the ability to *create* our lives as we wish. Society has bulldozed us into thinking that there is only one particular way of looking at things, be it scientific or spiritual, and that there are strict guidelines and dividing lines as to what's acceptable and what's not. We are afraid of accepting that there is no way to "know" any part of creation *fully*, because we can only observe an insignificant portion of any phenomena and that portion itself is subject to change. For our "knowledge" to be "superior" to aboriginal or medieval man's, our position in time and space would have to be superior — a concept we can easily dismiss as laughable.

We know no more about health, nature, or science than primitive man — we simply look at it from a different perspective and endlessly define the limited portion we can physically observe, completely ignoring the fact that we only observe a tiny symbolic fraction of the whole.

Many in the "New Age" movement have followed various trails seeking "enlightenment." They have many and various ideas — *aliens, spiritual channeling, crystals, harmonic convergence,* etc. — all supposedly the path to true spirituality. The New Age movement *has* opened a great doorway to mental expansion and experimentation, but generally has failed to live up to its promise. This is because most of its followers fail to understand that there is no "truth" or "real path" to enlightenment. It can be found anywhere and with any tools, in any situation.

If you, by following your inner guidance, are drawn to crystals or channeling or a church, then go! Open your arms to it and create! What must be understood, though, is that you don't have to *justify* your attraction to these concepts by *evaluating* them as the "truth" or as "real" for everyone. You just accept it as *necessary* for your growth at this *scale* and *position* in *your life,* and open yourself to the reality that you might discard this concept later on, granting yourself the ability to be continually *reborn.*

The world exists in reality only through what we perceive it to be. By redefining your life in terms that excite or fulfill you, you are giving that inner dynamic the ability to exhibit itself in the world. As long as you define the world as something concrete, defined, and immutable, you have encased that creative power within in a coffin, unable to affect the world.

U nderstanding the nature of creation unifies all religions and philosophies, because the symbolic manifestations that we perceive can have any number of interpretations. The different mental organisms that confound us can be called *evil spirits*, *the devil*, *mental disease*, *harmful influences*, *bad vibes*, *negative energy*, etc. Those that aid us can be called *angels*, the *Holy Ghost*, *confidence*, *mental health*, *inner guides*, etc. The Romans and Greeks had living entities that presided over everything imaginable, and they related to these entities and life in a very symbolic way.

Heroism is breaking those binding ideas away and defining the world as you see fit, realizing that the way you see the world is not a reflection of the world itself — it can be seen an infinite number of ways. The way you see the world is a reflection only of yourself and the inner forces at work. Since the world *is* only *what we observe of it*, by altering your perception you alter *it*. By stripping away your false evaluation and programming centers, the world "outside" *becomes a true reflection of your inner dynamic at work*, completely fulfilling and harmonious. Since "you" are a part of that world, you perceive yourself as completely in tune and at peace, fulfilling your inner dynamic.

Heroism is transcending the conflicting, dualistic evaluations of the world and moving into a realm where such considerations don't exist and your inner dynamic can be free to exhibit itself. This puts you in complete harmony with creation and removes the need for your system to be broken down and reorganized.

Heroism, or the fearless implementation of our perfect, harmonious inner dynamic, is the path to immortality, eternal life, and "salvation."

Lay then the axe to the root, and teach governments humanity. It is their sanguinary punishments which corrupt mankind.

— Tom Paine, *The Rights of Man*

The condition upon which God has given liberty to man is eternal vigilance; which condition if he break, servitude is at once the consequence of his crime.

— John Philpot Curran, 1750-1817

THE INDIVIDUAL
AND SOCIETY

Everywhere you turn in our society there is a boatload of experts on every subject, none of whom can seem to agree on anything. Because there are certain individuals who are socially-defined "masters" of certain lines of "knowledge" (doctors, psychologists, physicists, economists, attorneys, counselors, clergy, etc.), most of us feel inadequate, or unimportant, or unable to make any true impact on the world or even on our own lives. We feel we just do not have enough "knowledge," that we must run to the experts to tell us the road to happiness, or health, or wealth.

Our whole society worships the collection of knowledge, and has built great institutions and monuments to this form of education. Small wonder, since our society perpetuates itself through knowledge indoctrination, and has a much better grip on the individual the more thoroughly he or she is "trained." Society wants each of us to think that we cannot "succeed" in life without its knowledge, whether in the form of education or advice from highly educated experts.

That society's knowledge is false and transitory is easily observable. Our economists and doctors will be looked upon by future societies as shamans and witch doctors, just as we look back on past practitioners of the "learned arts" with humor and disgust. Remember, it wasn't so long ago that alchemy and astrology were "sciences."

This is the trap that individuals of every era fall victim to; they give the control of their lives over to the "experts." We don't want to take the responsibility for our existence, we want to justify and blame, to promote our self-worth and demean others. We don't want to face our inner problems and resolve conflict, we want to hide behind the curtain of social knowledge, which can be used to vindicate any action or position.

All knowledge is simply evaluations that are used to divide, justify, blame, and manipulate. It is inherently self-conflicting and transitory, and therefore meaningless. It must be dismissed so we can uncover our inner dynamic and implement it, and allow others to implement theirs without restriction or alteration. *Knowledge is the organic root of this diseased, destructive society,* and we must uproot it out of ourselves so we can harmonize with creation.

Being an equal part of creation, completely interconnected through the hierarchy of systems, and having been created perfectly as a symbolic manifestation with a perfect inner dynamic that is in complete harmony with the infinite universe, what is there that we are not in touch with? What true "knowledge" do we not have?

If we need healing, we are in touch with an infinite cauldron of entities and systems that can heal us instantly. If we need guidance, we are in touch with, are part of, and are constructed of a multiplicity of beings that can perfectly guide us and aid us. If we are poor, or troubled, or hurt, then what better source for aid than all of infinite creation?

For example, medical "knowledge" changes every few years, flip-flopping and reversing earlier views and procedures. Any doctor has about a 50-50 chance of administering the proper medication or procedure, because, let's face it, *anything* can happen. Wrong diagnosis, allergic reaction, carelessness, an accident, wrong dosage, misprint, wrong file, misunderstanding, side effects — you get the picture. Hell, no two doctors even have the same opinion on treatments, so your fate is up for grabs.

Doctors don't like to admit that they know little about the human body and its properties. They don't like to talk about the miracles that happen daily in spite of their dire predictions, or about the patients who die without cause. It shines too bright a light on the fact that their "knowledge" is worthless in and of itself, that there is far more going on than the mechanistic manipulation of body parts.

This is an example that can be applied to any area of "expertise" in life. I'm not saying that doctors should not be consulted, or that medication should not be taken. What I *am* saying is that your health is your responsibility, and control over it should not be given to a so-called "authority" on the subject, because there is only *one* authority on the subject of *your* health — you! You and the multiplicity of entities that are part of you and that you are part of, and the perfect inner dynamic that guides you. The proper treatment can only come when you manifest it or are guided to it, because every human body is different and has a different set of circumstances around it.

There are many books on these subjects; the above was just an example to demonstrate that we, as individuals, give society power over our lives when we subscribe to its knowledge and programming. We let it manifest health or sickness, wealth or poverty, happiness or despair in our lives based on its faulty, transient, self-contradictory "knowledge," instead of creating what we desire based on our perfect and harmonious *inner dynamic*, which is united with, created by, and *empowered* by the infinite Entity, or *God*.

No, the purpose of *this* book is to demonstrate the necessity of disposing of society's presence in our mind, because our minds are the soil from which it draws its sustenance. The time has come to evict its corrupt presence and let it die. If we do not, we will only sustain and empower its destructive presence, both in ourselves and in the world.

This book is also designed to give the individual the tools with which to do the job.

This above all: To thine own self be true.

— **Shakespeare,** *Hamlet*

ANARCHIC HARMONY

The universe was created to manifest perfection and complete harmony. To attain this, it creates all entities, at every position and scale, with an inner dynamic in perfect tune with the flowing, changing, *living* nature of the *hierarchy of systems*.

If all entities were able to implement their inner dynamic without hesitation, without alteration, then creation would surge into perfect harmony. The reason we do not perceive or accept this perfection is that we are too busy "knowing" that order must be maintained through restriction and suppression instead of freedom and liberty. Because we do not trust the natural order, we try to legislate and intimidate into existence that which we *think* should achieve balance and "proper" living.

Only the infinite, interconnected wisdom of creation *knows* what must be done to achieve harmony, and instills what is necessary of this knowledge into every part and sub-system of its being, when and where it is needed. Any sub-system, or entity, that assumes its knowledge is superior to that of another entity, and attempts to *convince* that entity of the superiority of its knowledge, is embarking on a path of disharmony and conflict, blinding itself with a colossal combination of *ignorance* and *arrogance*.

What any being perceives of creation is only an insignificant slice of the whole, and there is no "knowledge," "proof," or "evidence" that can be attained from it, *outside of the principles that govern every manifestation at every scale and position.*

In any arena of creation, a being looking at his surroundings would see *anarchy*, or an infinite cauldron of seemingly random events that have no real interconnectedness or meaning. A cell in our body would see total anarchy; we look into the physical world and see anarchy. Only when you move to a higher level of observation does the *harmony* created out of that *anarchy* become evident.

By accepting the obvious principles of reality, we unchain ourselves from the false knowledge and evaluations of society and *transcend* to an area that is able to observe the *anarchic harmony* of the living creation. We understand that all beings are uniquely created to fulfill a specific, living purpose. We understand that it doesn't matter what names or labels you put on the different forces, principles, and manifestations of creation; all such terms are only meant for the *individual* to choose freely in order to more easily demonstrate his or her inner dynamic, to make creation and all its wonders more accessible to them.

In the world, every entity has a different job to do so that a perfect balance can be maintained. This results in brilliant, vibrating harmony and untold beauty. In our bodies, each entity, each organ, each cell, each system — has a distinct duty to fulfill to maintain the divine harmony and beauty of the human body.

Order cannot be falsely instilled in any part of creation — it may last for a while, but eventually the living creation outgrows it. Harmony must come from within, from the individual expressions of the countless entities that creation manifests throughout itself.

Everything in creation is a living entity and has a living purpose, a perfect dynamic. This book, like every book (and everything else), is such an entity, and part of its purpose is to help individuals understand their position in creation, the importance of their existence, and to help them cut the chain that is dragging them down the whirlpool of destruction. By supporting the ineffective entity of society, we empower it to continue its diseased influence, corrupting more and more of the hierarchy of organic systems in our arena of creation.

It is our *duty* to renounce our mental allegiance to this corrupt society *and completely fulfill our inner dynamic*, without regard for the ramifications or consequences. Only then do we become perfectly effective in creation; only then can we find perfect harmony and joyous life, in tune and as one with the infinite Entity.

Call forth help and guidance from the infinite Entity and all the beings and manifestations around you, be they physical, mental, spiritual, or other. To receive understanding, though, one must first make the vessel clean by washing out all previous beliefs and "knowledge." The more you know, the less you can be taught.

Then, when this society passes, as it must, we will have the tools to survive that tumultuous time and will be prepared to nurture into life a new system, one that understands and follows the true structure and principles of reality.

YOU WILL ALSO WANT TO READ: